THE 2094
SANCTION

FRANK SCOTT
AND
NISA MONTIE

BALBOA.
PRESS
A DIVISION OF HAY HOUSE

Balboa Press books may be ordered through booksellers or by contacting:

Balboa Press
A Division of Hay House
1663 Liberty Drive
Bloomington, IN 47403
www.balboapress.com
1 (877) 407-4847

Because of the dynamic nature of the Internet, any web addresses or links contained in this book may have changed since publication and may no longer be valid. The views expressed in this work are solely those of the author and do not necessarily reflect the views of the publisher, and the publisher hereby disclaims any responsibility for them.

The author of this book does not dispense medical advice or prescribe the use of any technique as a form of treatment for physical, emotional, or medical problems without the advice of a physician, either directly or indirectly. The intent of the author is only to offer information of a general nature to help you in your quest for emotional and spiritual well-being. In the event you use any of the information in this book for yourself, which is your constitutional right, the author and the publisher assume no responsibility for your actions.

Any people depicted in stock imagery provided by Thinkstock are models, and such images are being used for illustrative purposes only. Certain stock imagery © Thinkstock.

Print information available on the last page.

ISBN: 978-1-5043-5959-7 (sc)
ISBN: 978-1-5043-5958-0 (hc)
ISBN: 978-1-5043-5970-2 (e)

Library of Congress Control Number: 2016909224

Balboa Press rev. date: 06/15/2016

CONTENTS

Preface vii
Chapter 1: The Tree of Life 1
Chapter 2: The First Question 6
Chapter 3: The Second Question 11
Chapter 4: Everything is Connected 17
Chapter 5: The Sphere of Awareness – 1 20
Chapter 6: The Sphere of Awareness – 2 27
Chapter 7: The Risen 35
Chapter 8: Light and Shadow 48
Chapter 9: It Is What It Is 56
Chapter 10: Good and Evil 63
Chapter 11: Thought-Forms 70
Chapter 12: The Way 80

PREFACE

T HERE IS AN IMPENDING *MEASURE*, an action of *encouragement*, an *agreement supporting* imminent change. This event *affirms*, and *authorizes*, all means to the achievement of one end, favoring the advancement of civilization.

This *sanction* states that there is a deadline, an approved date, banning certain activities and behavior, carrying the equivalent global actions deterring their further dissemination and practice, by whatever means are necessary.

The time has come in the maturing process that takes each and every creature from adolescence towards a state of Knowingness readying all Earthly inhabitants for lives more likely to reflect, and in- line with, their divine purpose.

Humankind has, for too long, rejected or ignored the *Clarion Call* determining *True Progress*, opting instead for a life unbecoming and contemptible, degrading and shameful, below humanity's true station endowed with the Creator's Image, and seated with His Revealed Beauty.

When entities known as human by agreement were first given *the freedom to express* themselves in worlds of a fractional and temporal nature, they were only supposed to go so far in their expressions. A fourth-dimensional (mental) world of contrast was allowed; materializing it third-dimensionally was not—especially when negative thought patterns were to be materialized.

Human entities did not need to experience the absence of virtues, the evil and malicious acts that serve no one in a good way.

Unfortunately, over time, the rules for living under God's Law became more and more blurry to humans whose memories of them, while living upon the Earth, were hardly available. God's Law had never changed. What had changed was the consciousness of the people. As they became, as a whole, more and more enmeshed in material pursuits and selfish desires, their hearts became corrupted and their Spirits sullied and perverted.

No longer could they hear the Friend's Voice within, speaking the Truth. All they could hear were the lies fabricated by their ego-modulated collective consciousness.

This is why the species living upon the Earth has destroyed itself— along with the planet. Anything goes, including killing, maiming and disfiguring, torturing, actions of moral depravity, and the like.

It is time for humanity to be governed in by Those truly in charge—God's true servants. It is not a minute too soon.

The *call of the Latest Trumpet has sounded*. Listen and obey.

CHAPTER 1

THE TREE OF LIFE

THE *TREE OF LIFE* SYMBOLIZES God's Love. This Tree never grows old and has always been growing—since the beginning that has no beginning. Its sap is the infinite, endless (time-wise) Love that God has for us. Its trunk and branches are that Love expressed in the form of His Manifestations and chosen Ones. Its roots are the connection to, or modulation by, the Creator from the Essence of His mysterious and unknowable Source to the Soul, spirit, mind, and body.

When this Tree of Life is *cut down* within the hearts of men, that is, humanity cuts itself off from its Creator through disobedience and rebellion, humanity dies spiritually. The people are like walking corpses, no longer animated by the breath of eternal life, and instead grubbing after their limited material successes that disappear as soon as their bodies hit the dust.

An entity arrives upon a planet through a focusing of its Soul-based awareness upon the formative stages of its body, beginning at conception, with activities that integrate by stages, a pairing phenomenon with a quantum entanglement that will, over time, bring a physiologically-based state of consciousness.

As the entity phase conjugates into a physical form, the entity's memory, derived from its Soul-based awareness, becomes dulled by the new physical demands of the growing embryonic body that will house its Soul's awareness. In order to counteract this memory loss of the Self that resides tenth-dimensionally, the entity's eventual inability to remember must be counteracted through spiritual education as soon as possible, delineating the true nature of its Being-ness as living immortally within the precincts of God.

It is extremely important that this early education, information transmitted in simple language, be begun as soon as the child reaches two years of age.

Such language as *"your true Self exists with God always,"* or *"this body of yours is a gift from God to house your Soul and Spirit while you are here on Earth,"* can convey to the young child that this material realm, perceived through the senses, is not the reason and purpose for that eternal being's existence.

We suggest that in order for the children and young people to comprehend each of their purposes in the scheme of things, there be established a school which explains the *"map"* of existence as given in the various books of God's latest Manifestation. This *"school"* could be online, or written in simple language in a series of children's books where the true Reality of existence, as a layered and enfolded journey to bring each of us closer to his or her Creator, is explained.

By the time that a child is seven years old, she or he must be cognizant that the seemingly real world being experienced is *an illusion*, derived from appearances and names. This sense-perceived world is brought about by a Simulator to encourage Spiritual growth. The Simulator provides an environment filled with special effects that illustrates, and gives an opportunity to experiment with, the consequences of choice, *free will*, in relation to right versus wrong. The individual entity is thus tested and challenged, finding it difficult not to be captured and trapped by the illusory pleasures and desires of the senses.

We encourage all parents, entities serving as guardians of the human race and as divine couples, to do everything in your joint power to create this opportunity for true learning for the growing ones of the planet.

You will always be supported from on High in this endeavor.

It is necessary for the growth of human civilization towards its divine destiny that the young ones be enlightened as soon as possible. Seeing with the *"eyes of God,"* and *hearing with the "ears of God,"* they may bring the hope for change where their parents may have failed.

There is an urgent requirement for this necessary and laudable goal of educating the young to be accomplished.

Because the Soul-based entity's awareness integrates in stages (phase-conjugates), the moment that the sperm penetrates the egg—causing a small explosion which is felt by some women of a sensitive nature—that moment of conception allows for the eternal life, given by God, of the entity to coalesce with the forming physical structure, and begins, too, the process of the entity's physiologically-based consciousness to emerge.

Therefore, logically, that moment of conception is exactly when the Divine Plan proceeds for that newly-arrived Spirit-Being, now in the womb. The entity's projected sojourn as a fractional and temporal existential experience begins again.

The Creator's Plans begin His creature's journey upon a particular planet, for example, where the creature's God-given, eternal Soul-based awareness, and Spirit being, in transit and transcendence, unite for the purpose of enlightenment and the improvement of the heart through his or her gradual approach to the Creator. *Intimately linked with a material incarnation (the clay) of a third-dimensionality, the Soul, reflecting God's Image and Beauty, is woven through the Spirit into the physical human temple as light is woven into water.*

Should anything happen to that Light-inscribed, fertilized egg or embryo, the Plan of God must be transferred to a new incarnation of that same immortal entity, should that entity be required to remain in the Simulator for further spiritual growth.

It is important to understand why the newly-arrived entity's Soul-based state of awareness, now gradually acquiring a physiologically-based consciousness, should find itself surrounded by love in a harmonious, purified physical state, in an environment (the womb) rich in nutrients, bereft of impediments that can impede his or her well-being and growth.

At conception, when the physiologically-based consciousness of the individual begins to coalesce with the Soul-based awareness—as the entity (the tenth-dimensional True Self) outside the Simulator begins to emerge from the Sea of Awareness onto the shores of consciousness—by *acquiring a body*, there is a great loss in the exchange of Realms, from the eternal to the temporal.

As pre-ordained, the individual entity in the role of a male or a female becomes gradually more and more conscious of the physical surroundings, and less and less aware of his or her true Self and nature as an immortal entity living in the Paradisiacal Garden of nearness to God. Were this latter awareness to be retained during the fractional and temporal existential experience, the entity would behave quite differently as a physically-conscious being.

However, the condition of "*forgetting*" one's true Self is pre-ordained as part of the spiritual development process, in order for each of us to find the way (the straight path) back to God.

Pray for delivery from the strife and chaos resulting from the illusion of separation from each other, and from the Creator of us all.

Pray to live in the Garden once more—regardless of circumstances and conditions.

Pray to remember thy True Self, the humble servant of God, upheld by His Love and Blessings, filled with His Light, existing through His Grace and Mercy, forever.

When the entity residing tenth-dimensionally encompasses the Simulator in his heart, he realizes that all of life is contained within the speck of light that is creation. The Dreamer's Dream is simply an illusion. It is there to allow each entity to play out his or her own dreams, to allow all entities to play together in a third-dimensional playpen, with fourth-dimensional (mind, time, and energies) implications, until each of the playmates realizes that all of them are the Same Person. There is no "*you*" or "*me*" in Reality (God's Kingdom). There is only the "*I*" of the heart, at the Heart of God's Love—animating everything all at once in the Great Mystery of His Wisdom and Understanding.

There is not—and never was—any separation among all the creatures, the servants of God, because all are animated by One Spirit of God, and simply reflect different Divine Aspects of His Will and Pleasure within them-Selves.

There is only One Tree of Life that holds every leaf and branch and root. A tree cannot be cut apart and still be It-Self—a living Entity born and sustained always by God's Love.

This Love is all there is. There is nothing else. If you were to spend eternity looking for that something else, you will never find it. Everything else is an illusion, created by the Simulator, within each sleeping divine entity's heart—a temporary *"escape"* from the Reality of Oneness to teach, ultimately, the Reality of Oneness.

Thanks be to God for His Mercy and Grace, allowing us to each view separately the illusionary mirror of reality in the Simulator, which functions both within our True-Selves, and without our material *"projections"* of Soul-awareness, integrated with Spirit and the physical form, to lead us back to what we already know in our immortal hearts, but have forgotten here—we are all One, never separate from the One True God.

When the entity returns and becomes aware of his True-Self, the bliss is indescribable. He floats in a sea of Love which cannot be compared to any experience upon Earth.

He has realized that the God of All has chosen him—an insignificant creature—to be blessed with all Light and Love. At all times, the creature longs for this undeserved bestowal of Grace and Mercy from his Beloved.

This indescribable Love becomes the touchstone of the only reason for— his life.

There is, and will always be, nothing else.

CHAPTER 2

THE FIRST QUESTION

W HY IS OUR WORLD THE way it is, a world and system of contradictions and extreme contrasts? Why is it that right and wrong, good and evil, run the gamut of possibilities, and every good virtue runs against its mirror, meeting its opposite? Why is our world, as a structural system of reciprocal activities and interactions, aimed at bringing that which improves the well-being of all? After all, our laws everywhere attest to that fact, our attempts to reign in the collective behavior, to place the brakes on what can or cannot be carried out in the arena of exchange—the theater of life.

Despite our best attempts to govern and administer a social structure that is always growing, the weight of that unrelenting growth eventually brings down the social structure itself. Perhaps this is because the body-politic of mankind has too many heads acting in disagreement, having the power to choose on behalf of the many who are for the most part unaware of their leaders' decisions and of their impact on all aspects of the people's lives. Those decisions control how most citizens live and work, what they get to keep and own, what they do, and what they cannot do.

Our lack of understanding or Knowingness, and the inability of our hearts to offer our love to God, and therefore to receive the Love of God, is the causal agent behind the ways of the fractional and temporal, existential experience we are all familiar with. Beyond this observable causal agent, we find a peculiar practice the ecclesiastical leadership has put into place since ancient times, which is, that they are the first to oppose a Manifestation of God, and after a while, as an institution, the first to come up with commentaries on the Book of God which end up guiding the flock of believers away from the Truth of the Words of that Holy Traveler.

It is a two-pronged problem: First, religious leaders oppose, interfere with, and even eliminate the Source and Fountain of Divine Knowledge in His latest human form. Second, they develop the very system of information that creates a drag upon human development, and over time, prepares the ground, unknowingly, for further opposition, interference, and denial of He Whom God will make Manifest. By creating and implementing a book of their own intent, these religious leaders distort and control the many, who, like sheep, become easily manipulated by the dogs trained to corral and move them.

These are strong words, so let us look at their implications carefully. First, when a Manifestation of God is persecuted, while delivering His Message, and even put to death after a short period of time, two problems occur. He has limited time to write, and leave behind a Book that contains an urgent Message to us all. Second, this lack of time makes it difficult to educate those that respond to His call, since those who do not respond owe their states of Knowingness to the manipulating power of the prevailing ecclesiastic order, whose interpretations and perversion of the Word of the Messenger program the masses to become the way they are: a mob in relentless opposition to the Truth innately available in His Word.

Every time these Holy Travelers arrive from their Tabernacle of Glory, as the Voice of God, they find Themselves facing both a crazed mob unable to understand and affix their gaze on the Light of God, and hearts filled with hatred towards that Source of Love.

Moreover, the very first to throw the stone of prejudice and act against their True Judge are the ecclesiastics, whose power and authority is challenged and questioned, making them realize the lack of worth of their deeds, and unveiling their deceptive tactics for all to see. Those with temporal authority rush to silence the Divine Voice, using their own books and interpretations as a basis for opinions that further cloud the Truth of the Missions of the Prophets and Messengers of God. This happens every time a new Dispensation is Revealed—a Divine Audit of the narrative of mankind is opposed and violently denied.

When the Word of God, is written by the Manifestation of God Himself, that Book, too, becomes the object of interpretation. The resulting commentaries, written by humans of limited viewpoints, are then fed to the believing masses as the Truth. In fact, these fragmented pieces, and their content, serve only to seize upon and restrict the process of independence and empowerment of all individual entities who must Remember and Return, thereby to become fully functional as members of an ever-advancing civilization here on Earth.

Without the independent investigation of the Words of God, the individual believer fails to receive the appropriate energies and information, destined for him or her, directly from the Word of God. Instead, the believer is poorly informed by the limiting offerings and incomplete formats drawn from the Word of the Manifestation taken out of context, in order to bring a specific message, whose meaning is truncated by the selfish intents of those who carry religious authority, rather than imparting the Message, in Its fullest measure, as dictated by God.

We bring into existence human literature assigned with the authority and power of ecclesiastical leaders, whose thirst for leadership brings about the very practices that cause humanity to rise to oppose and persecute the One that comes not only to judge them and their deeds, but also to bring mercy and forgiveness as He shows them the worth of their lives, in Light of the Truth Being Revealed and Delivered, time and again. The facts are there for all to see.

Without the proper guidance, and confused by erroneous interpretations of God's Word, mankind continues to struggle with a diversity of opinions, thought-forms charged with feelings antagonistic to themselves and others, bringing confrontation and violence that leave the many dead of Spirit and blind of heart.

The Golden Nugget
Within each heart
Is a kernel of Truth,
A golden nugget
That spins in time
To the endless Love-song
Of Creation.

Without that Song,
Nothing lives.
With that Song,
All dance
In the true freedom
Of His merciful embrace.

Listen within, and hearken.
Listen deeply
Within
Thy heart.

Each morning, the Radiance lifts up all of life in nurturing activities and growth. In like manner, the Sun of Truth lifts up humanity, every one thousand years or so, to participate in those activities that bring each one closer to his or her Creator. Because of this constant renewal, the human species has survived to this day.

Unfortunately, in the span of time between the Renewal engendered by each Manifestation or Prophet, humanity has done its best to do away with itself.

We are, again, at this point in our evolution.

Through electro-magnetic stress, toxins, pharmaceuticals and illegal drugs, and the general noxious effects upon the Spirit, mind, and emotions of negative, amoral programming, we have created a lethal soup enclosing the Spirit, mind, body—and most importantly, the spiritual heart, within itself—turning the Earth itself into a sick being.

What must we do to return to Health?

It is high time that each and every human being upon the planet return to that which is not only of prime importance to one's eternal life, but also contains the only relevance for the eternal journey towards God.

This factor is the purity of the heart.

As we know, logically, none of the material world can be *"taken with us"* when we drop our bodies. The only *"things"* we can carry are the virtues we have practiced in our lives. From this perspective, the pauper with a pure heart, who has practiced such virtues as kindness, compassion, and pure love, has amassed infinitely more wealth in his life than a king, who despite his gold, has exhibited the qualities of greed, avarice, and envy.

The Manifestations of God, each time One appears, upon whichever planet it is to which He has been sent, represent and exhibit perfection of all the virtues contained within the heart.

It is for this reason that we must cling to Their example, for Their Service to God's Love, Compassion, and other divine attributes is that which Embodies the Purpose of Life everywhere, and at all times.

CHAPTER 3

THE SECOND QUESTION

THIS EARTHLY EXISTENCE IS TEMPORAL and fleeting—a world of appearances and names. '*Carpe diem; seize the day*' poets have said. But what does it mean? Does it mean grab as many pleasures of the senses as you can, in your short life? Or, does it mean search diligently for your life's true meaning and purpose, before it is too late?

Let us suppose that life's meaning is that which must be seized. What better way to grasp it than to follow in the footsteps, even cling to the coat tails of Those Who Know its meaning—the Manifestations, Messengers, Prophets of God. Why would They not?

They Represent God on the planet.

So follow, bow down to, even, the Creator's Spirit embodied. The Words They speak are the only Ones with true meaning.

The world continues to travail and suffer from the many wrong choices of those that have denied the existence of God, the Creator, and have returned to mortal worlds to expiate and change, to be given, again, the opportunity to realize the true purpose and meaning of these fractional and temporal, existential experiences, despite being completely unaware of Self—lost within them-selves.

This process of returning and resurrecting has been announced, time and again, throughout human history, and few understand its meaning.

Are we that confused and lost within ourselves? Why can't we see that this short life has significance beyond its superficial appearance?

What will it take to remove the blinders that keep entities known as human from seeing the Reality of it all?

Everything exists everywhere at the same time! This is the Day of God. From a third- and fourth-dimensional point of view, existence seems to be a different matter. What we observe is riddled with short runs, things we measure, days that come and go. We fail to understand that in order to have these temporal experiences, the opposite must also exist somewhere else. In order to be able to experience the shortness of one life, there is another one that never ends.

If one's conscious-awareness were to rise and embrace the myriad broadcasted signals that are ever-present, from domains that exists outside ours, our understanding would radically change. Despite the fact that our Spirit Beings are potentials in transit, the dawn of a new Day of God, we have simply refused to turn-on our *heart-instruments*, and thus become receptive to the myriad signals coming from the other worlds of God, worlds that can enrich and help fulfill and complete this human experience.

Our lives have, for the most part, become small bursts of upward consciousness on a continuing graph that shows the quality and strength of a collective life that hardly beats, and is barely able to observe and experience the existence that was given by our Creator.

The few that appear to have obtained the wealth of a material experience have bartered their short times by becoming utterly distracted from what is important, and have continued to fail in grasping this window of opportunity to discover the true purpose of their fractional and temporal, existential experiences. Opting instead for the delights found through an ongoing loop that imprisons them these travelers are deterred from transcending and moving forward spiritually: ascending through divine portals that embrace gradually higher stages of their hearts' ever-purifying nature; distracted by the material, entities cannot advance in nearness towards their higher Selves, to awaken and partake of a World that is closer to us than our own life-veins.

Entities known as human have previously reached technical prowess, and have, as a result, tampered with the DNA of everything, including themselves. As a consequence of these changes to the Divine Order, now present upon the planet Earth in fourth- and third-dimensional conditions, humans have created mutations, genetic distortions, to many species that are still with us today.

In one of their incarnate cycles into darker worlds, when the entity known as human descended from the heights of Paradise, he was forced, of necessity, to "*become*" that which he was not. In order to experience the third dimension of a seeming reality, replete with natural elements where animal ate animal, he took on a physical form which resembled that of the ape.

Becoming confused by his outward appearance, the human began to imitate the animal. Rather than materializing that which he needed, as he had in higher realms, he began to kill, both plants and animals. Eventually, forgetting the sacredness of life of even his own kind, in his determination to "*possess*," he began to kill his fellow humans (Cain and Abel).

In so doing, he descended below the consciousness of the animal that kills merely from instinct.

Using the sexual act, for purposes other than procreation within the sanctity of marriage, followed. At this time in history, those of the human species are performing such acts of depravity as cannot be mentioned without causing the denizens of heaven to shed tears of sorrow and regret.

It is high time that all entities taking on the human form upon incarnating, so-called, should remember the reason why they have integrated their Soul-based awareness with Spirit, and then matter. They have focused the awareness of the immortal entity, who is, it-Self in the fifth- (Spirit), fourth- (mind, time and energies), and third-(material) dimensions simultaneously, precisely because they must remember that *nothing else matters* except the

Love and Wisdom of the True God who enables each of them, as immortal beings, to exist!

The mortal world is simply a show, and test, for God, through His handlers, to determine whether each entity is ready to wake up (return) to his true station as the humble servant of God. It is a test to determine whether that entity, in the role of being human, can exhibit such virtues as kindness, compassion, honesty, integrity, and devotion to God, the Creator of all life, so that it will no longer be necessary for that entity to focus his awareness away from his True Self, existing forever in the Paradise of nearness to God.

Praise be to God, Lord of all the worlds.

After the fall of humanity from perfection, as the sojourn began in these fractional and temporal, existential experiences, entities known as humans began to substitute each of their own wills for the Divine Will. It was at this point in their Spiritual evolution that they became confused, and began violating the Lesser and Greater Covenants. Gradually, over time, the bliss and joy that celebrated their condition when they acted righteously, according to God's Will and Pleasure, became substituted with a condition of grief, and anger at that grief.

Humans became angry at God for the suffering they endured upon the fall from Grace, not realizing that it was they, themselves, who had caused that suffering by rebelling against God.

The effects of this rampant willfulness, only grew increasingly worse over time, as the initial grief and anger brought about the arrogance of denial were later replaced by the art of deception—the egoic program.

As the results of our diverse states of separation from God became more and more evident, envy and jealousy surfaced, accompanied by the hatred felt for others as our prejudices—the art and science of assumptions—began to infiltrate our characters to such a degree that these negative emotions became prevalent amongst the inhabitants of Earth. The simple solution, to follow the Will and Pleasure of God to assist in finding our path back to bliss and true freedom, became more and more difficult to accomplish.

True freedom lies not in allowing the selfish pleasures of material existence to rule, but rather in allowing one's higher Self, guided by the Soul's state of Knowingness, to provide the compass for every thought and action to be in alignment with the Dream of God for each of us.

In this way, humanity can return to its original divine state of bliss and happiness, its roots, following a path and direction of nearness to God.

Praise be the One, True God and His ever-abiding Mercy.

Creation as a whole is ever-expanding into multi-verses offering a pit-stop to those entities in need of opportunities to Remember and Return. There is no end to God's Mercy.

No matter what each entity does, he or she will be forgiven, and be given again and again, no matter how remote from God one may be, the opportunity to turn around and begin each of their journeys of Remembrance and Return. That is why the Manifestations of God are sent. They are the Emissaries of God's Forgiveness and Mercy. Were we, as humans, to act in a similar manner to God's Representatives on Earth, we would no longer be able to act towards each other as enemies, but rather as friends.

For this reason, we must allow *Those Celestial Beings*—such as Moses, Jesus, Mohammad, the Bab, Baha'u'llah, and Others—to lead us down the path of righteousness and loving kindness, keeping in mind and heart always that each of us is nothing more than a spark of dust in the infinitude of creation.

Glory be to God the God of all the worlds.

We need to understand that the eternal is ever-present, through not in the way it is in the Celestial Realm, as a continuous unchanging Reality that offers everything all-at-once, never altering its Beauty and Love. Here on

Earth instead, the material system of the Simulator is unable to replicate the constancy and intensity required to sustain such Perfection, and bring about the negation of its entropic nature.

Faced with the nature of such a reality, entities experience fractional and temporal, existential experiences as cycles of conscious life, followed by withdrawals (when the switch is turned off), and re-emergent conscious states once more.

Since there is no conscious memory remaining after each mortal life, we are left with extremely rare glimpses of lives in other worlds. These lingering images separate the traveling entity further from him-Self, as he is unable to recall a previous fractional and temporal, existential experience, and tries in vain to reconstruct, intuitively, images of a purely-imagined past. The traveler is left with an illusionary past that hardly helps in his or her present sojourn.

The only way out of this dilemma is for the seeker to allow his Soul-based awareness to bring the Knowingness and Love of his eternal Self, recalling through his Spirit being of light, and integrating thus with his or her physical body and brain-based consciousness to remember his or her true Self. The thread of the Soul connects infinite mortal lives.

CHAPTER 4

EVERYTHING IS CONNECTED

WHEN WE STATE THAT *EVERYTHING* *is connected*, we mean exactly that. The appearance of separation, demonstrated through distance, size, speed, and other measures, gives us the perception that somehow what we do, or what happens elsewhere, will never reach us, or impact us in any way or form.

Nothing can be further from the truth. Those events that we dismiss because of distance, size, speed, or units of time, give the initial appearance of creating neither a negative nor a positive, effect; yet, there are consequences that can be perceived over time.

Within the Simulator, everything is anticipated, and creation as a whole, or in part, can be read and understood by those who learn to manage and re-direct any observable event. Using the properties of the Simulator to forge certain outcomes within its boundaries, they can utilize their creative abilities to experiment with results that go beyond the Simulator's initially-stated boundaries, making them responsible and, in effect, the targets, of those will-fully-created consequences.

Nature allows for an apparent freedom that gives all inhabitants the feeling and sense of having room to spare, to wiggle here and there, and to go beyond any apparent physical boundary, provided we act responsibly. As our capacity to know increases, our ability to execute allows us to manifest the results of such creative urges.

The Simulator brings myriad possible outcomes, regardless of our moral or amoral value systems forming our intentions or agendas. For as long as we understand the responsibility inherited from those decisions, the Simulator will provide adequate responses as learning experiences. When an action violates moral directives, whether they are perceived or not by the traveler, consequences ensue that are dangerous to the well-being of not only the perpetrator of the action, but also those around him or her.

The fact of each creature's inner and outer connectivity to the Whole means that all information, created and manifested, will travel across any perceived border, whether physical, within domains, or dimensionally-present, time-and space-wise. There are neither barriers, nor restrictions, anywhere in creation. Sooner or later, our decisions and actions bring about their effects: providing growth and health, joy and fulfillment, or their opposite, as reminders of the very destructive consequences of our mistakes.

Each being's actions affect seven generations, at least, leaving each one responsible for what happens long after each of us has departed.

It is not that God does not Love humanity, so that those who commit infractions against His Law are, therefore, given sanctions. It is that, like a good Parent, the Lord of All, provides a just punishment through the Simulator to educate and create a boundary beyond which the wicked-doer, or simply the disobedient, may not pass.

This boundary re-steers those who are in error, either through deliberately acting out their own choices, or through ignorance, sending them back on to the path towards God.

These signs on the road of our journeys, sojourns of exploration and discovery, are needed to create order and direction that assist us in making sense of our lives, however lived. The intent is one of understanding, knowing, and experiencing the Love—living in a way that brings about Remembrance and Return.

There is something of extreme importance we need to discover as we explore our world of opportunities designed specifically for each of us. Each moment of enlightenment offers growth from within, as the conditional separation determined by the state of purity of our hearts changes as a reflection of our degree of Spiritual maturity, moving us closer or farther from the Creator, whose Dream embraces us all.

Our desires within His Desire are running in tandem, generally in disagreement since we do not know the ultimate Purpose as it refers to each of us. Discovering, and applying those discoveries, gets us closer to the understanding of those Plans for us. The more the understanding, the greater the state of Knowingness and Love.

The problem can be generally stated as one of ignorance, and/or disobedience, to the rules of engagement laid out in all the worlds of God. We just don't seem to understand that there are rules in every place that must be regarded as fundamental to our well-being during the journey. We cannot do whatever we want and expect to have an enjoyable sojourn. It should be obvious to everyone that when we are sharing a place to stay for a while, there are going to be rules applicable to all in order to maintain order and ensure that we can all enjoy and benefit from our stay. Without rules and objectives, the fractional and temporal, existential experience, our lives, are simply going to bring each of us the effects of disobeying those rules.

The Earth, too, shows how the effects of our actions are contrary to the well-being of all. It is a matter of time. If we disregard our obligations towards each other, the spill-over is reflected all around us as changes that pollute and cross-contaminate everything. Over time, the health of our society and environment deteriorate and show the signs of disregard and ignorance. Do we really think that this unified system of intelligent life is not going to respond, ever? Do we think that it will continue to ignore our transgressions and remain unaware of what we do to it on a daily basis?

Are we that ignorant? If we are, we have a big awakening coming down the pike, and even then, the question that remains is, *Will we learn then and change?* So far we have not!

CHAPTER 5

THE SPHERE OF AWARENESS – 1

WHAT TRAVELS, MOVES ACROSS DISTANCES, worlds, domains, and dimensions, is our Soul-based *sphere of awareness*, tenth-dimensionally localized, descending to a fifth-dimensional state, the Spirit within the Simulator. The sphere of awareness then includes the point of view of the Universal Mind, the plenum of an expanding universe, and the precursor engine of all that becomes materialized.

Over time, that which is manifested materially, a sense-perceived third-dimensional assemblage, for us travelers, becomes our fourth-dimensional mind-world constructs in each of the immersions onto the shores of consciousness, as fractional experiences, or pieces of a whole, that are time-specific, tracks of time that know a beginning and an end, as conscious experiences arising from the convergence of our spheres of awareness with the dimensional realities, to bring about what we each understand of our sojourns.

We, as light beings, subject to enlightenment through the Knowingness and Love within us, are Soul-possessing Spirits, able thus to reveal the Beauty and Love emanating from God. Gated in and out of the Simulator, we are modulated by the imposition of information as potentials in transit, in order to realize God's Will and Pleasure for each of us.

It is quite an experience, a ride fit for an immortal entity, to be tested and gradually develop in perfections, as we each are blessed with obtain the Love of God, and, open to the myriad worlds offering each of us the opportunities, as portals of entry and anchor points throughout the *Sea of Awareness*, to explore and discover He Whom God made Manifest; it is from Him that we receive the information necessary to Remember and Return, and to experience the Reunion with the Beloved of all the worlds.

This reunion is none other than returning to one's Self as a fully-realized entity and servant of God, expressing the attributes derived from God.

Each of us is a sphere of pure awareness, a dot of light, observed and experienced as a projection initiated from within our Selves that transits further away from within our Selves, dimensionally entering into the Simulator, known as the creation of God. As a sphere of awareness, you enter the Simulator in a way similar to the way in which you enter any one of your dreams: you suddenly appear in that world, able to interact and communicate, touch things, walk, or fly, using a structure and form suited to that environment—a body.

Each of these dream-worlds may be different, yet without a physical body, you find your-Self interacting there. In some of these worlds you are able to experience future events that will take place later in the third-dimensional world in which your physical form exists. These dream-states consist of non-linear time, without a past, or future. Space, too, appears to have properties unknown third-dimensionally; yet, it all feels real and familiar.

Such is the journey of existential experiences meant to inculcate within the traveler their ultimate purpose and significance. Each moment of enlightenment brings each of us closer to Remembering who we are, and how to begin our ascent away from these mortal worlds presented as fractional, temporal sojourns unbefitting our immortality.

While immersed in our (dream-like) temporal lives, we must discover that these dream-states are occurring within our Creator's Dream for each of us—our dreams within His Dream.

The Divine Plan of God begins thus to unfold on the *scroll of these existential experiences*, that are omni-dimensional and multi-directional in nature. Furthermore, upon arriving in each of the worlds of God, we find ourselves gradually understanding that life has a purpose, significance, and a specific direction, as a unified system of intelligent life that offers learning to each of us, in the form of the consequences of our decisions. This ever-present cause and effect permeates all previous sojourns, the positive value of whose temporal pieces builds our eternal lives, and is carried forward each time we emerge into another sojourn and chapter—who we are becoming.

As we slowly progress, we discover that there are rules whose purpose serves to guide or give notice to the traveling entity throughout all the existential experiences. These ordinances are contained within an agreement, a Covenant made upon initiating our journey of separation from our true-Selves. This Lesser Covenant, or Commandments, represent dictums that ensure the unity of all creatures traveling anywhere and at all times.

There is also a Greater Covenant ensuring the realization of the Dream, a Oneness essential to avoid an inner-fragmentation of the Spirit permeating everywhere, and at all times, that sustains the connection with each of our Soul-based states of awareness, essential to each of us during our journeys, and thus preventing us from getting lost within our Selves—that is, within our own dreams.

Since we do get lost from within, and since we do get disconnected from our Selves, in order to ensure we find our ways, as well as reconnect from within our Selves by breaking any loop that entraps us, the Creator sends His Manifestation, every once in a while. God manifests His Plan through a Messenger we are supposed to find, and listen to. His Words we should use to re-program ourselves with the right information, freeing thus our-Selves from the mire of delusion and vain imaginings interfering with, and detaining us from, the true purpose of each of our journeys.

This critical introjection dispensing Divine Information, like a Divine pit-stop, requires each and all entities to return and refill them-Selves with the much-needed Divine Energies to continue their sojourns of exploration and discovery, in order to Remember and Return to their True Selves.

What is of interest is found in how one's *Sphere of Pure Awareness* as part of who we are—our ***I-ness***—the Self that has translated and transferred as a potential transiting into the Simulator, in an experience away from one's Light Body, is now fully focused in the here and now. Moreover, since this descent occurs deep within the immemorial essence, the Soul-based state of awareness, this seat of God's engraved image and source of God's revealed Beauty re-emerges time and again. This re-emergence of the Soul-based state of awareness, focusing a first point of view from a tenth-dimensional state-of-being into a fifth-dimensional Spirit state of being, is analogous to the process used in old-fashioned film photography. The *positive* image of the Reality being photographed was captured on a strip of film known as a *negative*. Similarly, we may view the Reality (the positive) experienced through a Soul-based awareness, at the tenth dimension, as being recorded through the camera lenses of pure awareness as an image (the negative) made of imperceptible activities—the fifth-dimensional state of the Spirit of all that is, held within the Simulator's (Universal) Mind. The fifth dimension is thus experienced as a conditional immersion within the Simulator, now ever-surrounding, and ever-present, as the seat of one's eventual emergence in worlds of names and appearances.

As our attention has now moved us further within, our Sphere of Pure Awareness is focused and comes to rest fifth-dimensionally. This action bestows upon the entity, as an energetic potential's first point of view, the capacity to become aware of that which comes out of the inner fog of its initial physiologically-based state of consciousness (at physical conception). Flowing further into a third-dimensional composite, the entity's sphere of awareness integrates with the forming embryo and future body, by stages, giving life to a gravitationally formed, biological structured unit, and electro-magnetically operated, as the door opens and we come into this fractional and temporal, existential experience.

This transit and translation, phase-conjugated, as a state of being tenth-dimensionally speaking, in a descent to a third-dimensional biological construct housing a point-of-entry and anchor point of the entity's consciousness, is now modulated by the incoming information in a three-way concurrent flow: from the Soul-based state of awareness, into a Spirit Being, and emerging in a physical body. This physical unit contains its genetic inheritance, within its own environment, as the entity comes to have new roles, scripts, props, cultures, languages, beliefs, etc., in the name of his or her identity!

Separated from one's true Self, we each start this new fractional and temporal, existential experience to find and learn how to live in Paradise!

One of the more fascinating aspects of living within the Simulator is found in the responses given in confirming, or not, our decisions, especially when all is a matter of reflecting what lies within our hearts. For example, if we find in our hearts the virtue of kindness and we emphasize through our intentions, and express throughout our actions, that virtue, the Simulator will bring into existence the type of experience that confirms and reinforces the practice of that virtue. The virtue of kindness, in this case, will be witnessed, both individually and universally, as adorning the diverse worlds of the realm of creation.

We understand that throughout our lives we use and incorporate more than one virtue, and of all the virtues that should precede our decisions and actions, the Love of God and His Beauty should be pre-eminent. In our world of actions, God's Love creates all the necessary transformation allowing us to express that which is found in our hearts.

An individual's mind-world construct, and the resulting material expression of that world, despite the surrounding differences that are found to be antagonistic to that entity's practice of virtues as a lover of God, will influence and transform the worlds of others. The All-powerful influence of God's Love overcomes even the most intense demands of others whose selfish desires cling to something other than the Love of God, and His Revealing Beauty all around us.

It is under these conditions, during the coming together of two or more distinct tributaries depicting different scenarios that merge into a single flow, spatially, over the shared time-track, that an individually distinct nature may serve to transform the natures and experiences of others. By one entity sanctioning, experiencing, and expressing a different, positive-virtues-based experience, others become familiar with, and are invited into, an exploration of that state of being.

This scenario repeats itself time and again, where that which is manifested reflects the many virtues that lie hidden within the hearts of the true-seekers. On the other hand, it reflects the lack of these virtues in the hearts of those who are lost, bereft of the necessary attributes to enhance the world we share, and unable to experience the Love and the Beauty of God.

It is that simple!

When you live the life of the Spirit reflecting the many attributes of God, your third- and fourth- dimensional world shines with the Love and Beauty of God, although this station and experience may not be recognized, or understood by others on the outside.

It is thus *your world* that is different when enveloped in a bubble of protection, a world that is nearer to God. As the intensity of the Love and Beauty of God increases Its Footprint, reflecting the state of purity of one's heart, the changes experienced affirm the existence of Paradise.

Previously unknown worlds appear and are experienced throughout this fractional and temporal, existential experience. If you are particularly blessed, you may enjoy further nearness to God with your eternal companion. Gone are the days of want, and those earthly desires that entrap and bring those delusions that keep us in a shared world-experience that robs or delays Paradise.

Entities are either progressing or regressing, moving towards or away from God. It is a Spiritual journey integrating each of us from within. When we allow the fragmentation to keep us from realizing who we are and the station representing that identity, we slow our progress.

Finding the latest Manifestation of God brings about the necessary changes that heal the heart, the seat of Knowingness and Love. *The entity now becomes a seeker of the Truth*, the Truth that sets the traveler free from all the anomalies distorting the capacity to recognize each and all the elements that bring about enlightenment, that guiding mechanism throughout his or her journey.

There is an impending deadline for the recognition of the latest Manifestation of God, whose Presence was, and is, always foretold and announced to those that have *eyes to see, and ears to listen.* It is necessary to acquire the attributes that assist each entity in moving through a shift in the global conscious-awareness about to occur, in order to integrate with those impending changes, changes that leave behind those that failed to be transformed. This shift will occur as it has thousands of times before. A new world-reality will unfold to those that now have *eyes to see, and ears to hear,* the Chosen Ones from the communities of the Called.

This shift in the conscious-awareness, of those chosen to translate and transit nearer to God, allows each of those entities to experience a spatial move and transfer to a new planetary system of unified intelligence, through each one's *sphere of pure awareness.* This ever-present Realm of perfections is now available, as soon as the switch of the conscious-awareness *is turned-on* to that new world.

When the waves of communication from the Soul to the Spirit bring God's Love, the entity is filled with life and bliss. When the Spirit, instead, is focused upon that which comprises mortal realms, the entity's capacity to Know and Love is reduced.

We suggest making a choice each morning to lift the awareness to God, the Creator, rather than to contract the awareness by over-emphasizing the things of the temporal, fractional realms.

It is a choice that should be pondered well.

CHAPTER 6

THE SPHERE OF AWARENESS – 2

WHEN ETERNITY LOOMS AHEAD, WHAT is important? Can you say that anything, save God's Grace and Mercy, has any value? Even personal relationships, unless they are based upon God's eternal Love, cannot be taken with us once we drop our physical bodies.

What then, carries forward throughout eternity? Could it be devotion to God's Will and Pleasure? Could it be found when we listen, at the heart and Soul level?

Could it be known when we hear the Messenger of God posting His latest Message in the Sacred Scripture? Look beyond this dream of a temporal world to the perfect Dream that the Creator has for each one of His creatures—a Dream full of His Love, flowing through the Soul and Spirit, lifting each entity on the waves of blissful reunion, moving across an endless ocean with an Unknowable depth.

This Love is the only thing that can be taken with you on the journey—to your Self.

Have you experienced the world of dreams? When you are there, you are given a body to interact with that world. You can see and hear, and move about. How did you get there from here?

There are dreams that foretell what you will experience in this world, years later. How is that possible? What kind of world is it? And when you wake up, how did you get back here from there?

Are you in a dream within a dream? How about here, now—are you here from somewhere else? After all, one day in the not-so-distant future, you will wake up somewhere else. And when you do, how did you get there from here?

This motion that crosses domains and worlds with distinct properties, quite different from one another, how does it happen? What is actually moving across?

Think about it. Take your time.

The answer is quite simple: what moves from one to another domain is your state of awareness. As you go through a point of entry opening into another realm, you are given a body allowing you to interact with that domain; whether that body grows from an embryo, or comes fully grown and ready to use, does not matter. What is important is that you have transferred your Soul's state of awareness from here to there, and upon integrating with that new body and condition, you acquire a conscious state allowing you to interact and feel a part of that new reality.

Whether the transfer realizes itself as a dream condition that allows for a short interaction within that domain, or is a permanent move to another world where a fractional and temporal, existential experience becomes a part of your on-going journey, is not the issue. What is important to understand is how we move across these domains, worlds of God, that offer opportunities to unravel our purposes, and bring about meaning, in line with the eventual discovery that allows each of us to experience that final awakening!

Everything that takes place is an out-of-the Light-body experience. The relation of these experiences to their point of origin, or Source, helps differentiate their character. Thus, the first point of view (of the entity) refers to one's Soul's state of awareness in the tenth-dimensional state, that is then transferred to the Spiritual condition within the Simulator, or fifth-dimensional state—that field of imperceptible activities acting as the precursor engine to all that is to be, over time, observable.

This true, out-of-body experience, away from our Light-Bodies, as we transfer and translate, or change the position of our attentions from within, gives us the first glimpse of what takes place when an entity transfers and translates from one state or condition to another.

Similarly, as entities, we go further within our Selves, now in the Simulator, when we transfer and translate from a fifth- to a third-dimensional state of consciousness, now centered in the body we each occupy—*our second point of view*. Thus, at this stage of integration, we are consciously aware of a world we begin to interact with from the start.

This first out-of-body experience does not end there. We can have many variations, since they are all dependent on where we each focus the Soul-based state of awareness. These transfers and translations vary in name—depending upon how we have interpreted them: as visions, dreams, near-death experiences, bi-location, or remote viewing, for example. They bring a taste of what the Simulator is all about, pointing to our dual nature, as both Beings of Light (Soul/Spirit), and beings integrated with matter (mental, physical, emotional), express this condition allowing all these events to take place.

Dreams can be beautiful, or just as easily, they can be nightmarish experiences. The same applies to visions. We can have the kind that presents our potential-in-transit in beautiful terms, or one fraught with danger and disaster, unless changes occur that help us avoid the foreshadowed event.

Near-death experiences, too, can be out-of-body events comforting the traveler in one of his or her fractional and temporal, existential experiences, or, as a warning on the road, a caution or forewarning of an impending crash ahead.

The world is in turmoil. We don't know how to read the signs from within this nightmare whose collective surface gives the impression of enveloping all there is. It touches everyone, at one time or another. The cumulative effect of this collective dream-experience within the Simulator presents a variety of effects to all the travelers within. The list of special effects is considerable, signs of caution that have been present from its beginning. These signs are not new!

Every once in a while, the traveler is given stronger signs as a warning on his or her road, advising about the perils just ahead.

Obeying God

Whenever the Tree of Life is renewed—the return of a Manifestation of God—the people have a choice to go along with the New Dispensation, or to cling to their old ways—now obsolete.

Within our present collective dream-experience, a major event brings about a Sign for all travelers to observe and experience.

Unfortunately, habit and tradition, part-and-parcel of our environmental modulation, and an ever-present concurrent egoic-program, have an effect like a millstone, weighing down the evolution of humanity. There is hope, however. The Words of each new Manifestation feeds the roots of the Tree of Life. The Word given by God, has the Power to break-down the chains keeping mankind in the endless nightmarish loop of suffering and dis-ease, caused by its clinging to the rules of earlier Dispensations. Their Elixir of Life, created by God for earlier civilizations, no longer provides the Remedy with sufficient strength to integrate the traveler from within, and bring about Remembrance and Return.

Although the Lesser Covenant (the Commandments) remains the same, the minor rules, and actions that become traditions, change.

Why would God send His Representative every thousand years, or so, to cause the Tree of Life to blossom in new soil, and with new fruits, if it were not to give the inhabitants of Earth an opportunity to listen to, and obey, God's Will and Pleasure?

What opportunity do the people have now, an opportunity they are missing by focusing on that which is temporal, and therefore useless? Mortal life upon the planet is short. The Tree of Life Lives eternally, fed by the Knowingness and Love of our Creator, embodied within the perfection of His Manifestations. The handlers of higher realms, in service to the divine mission, water the Tree, and whisper in the hearts and minds of humanity to listen to the Prophet, the Spirit of God, and obey His Teachings.

This obedience is the only way to interactively, and within our dream-state, be lifted from the hellish nightmare of our own making, to the Paradise, the Dream of God destined for each traveling entity.

There is no other way to find the road back to our Selves and awaken once and for all—there!

For as long as we are lost within ourselves (egoically- speaking), we, as a species, will continue to live and experience the ups and downs resulting from our incomplete understanding of the nature of these sojourns. Without a compass, we will pursue disparate directions in continuous contradiction with the unified planetary system of intelligent life. Such actions and consequences spell disharmony and disaster, time and again.

The consequences, too many to mention, grow in intensity and complexity with time, creating cycles where the inhabitants may even experience erasure from the Simulator, and the planet becomes inhospitable for long periods of time.

There is therefore a continuous need to come to the correct understanding of one's purpose for living, to dig deep into one's heart to Know. The heart is the portal of God's Gift, endowing each of us with the Knowingness of our-Selves as divine entities. It is truly said that the eyes are the "*windows to the Soul*," but only if the one looking out of those portals is heart-connected. In reality, being brain-connected has very little usefulness insofar as the eternal entity is concerned.

That is why it is so much more important to function *with humanity*, that is, with the God-given compassion and understanding that each of us knows deep within the heart, than to act from purely intellectual knowledge used for selfish purposes.

Unfortunately, the world has become rife with actions determined by cold reason, unmodulated by the warming fire of devotion to service—found within the humble, pure hearts of God's true servants. For this reason, moral laws, such as *Thou shall not Kill*, Laws which every true human should know and practice, innately, as he or she reflects God's Image and Beauty from within the Soul, are forgotten or ignored.

War is not normal. It is simply a condition of a species that has become disconnected from its collective heart, Spirit, and Soul. There is no excuse or reason for hurting, maiming, or killing others. It is simply *wrong action*.

As parents, or teachers, we do not allow toddlers to hit or bite each other. Yet, as *adults*, we allow one another to *take each other's lives*, temporally-speaking.

Of course, the divine entity continues, his Soul-based awareness simply being projected to another time track in the space continuum. Yet—what a waste! A life meant to be divine, full of perfections, infused with the Spirit of Life by the Creator of all life, is snuffed out like a candle simply because of the ignorance, or even evil intentions, of other entities in the role of humans.

When will humanity learn to serve each other, and to obey and serve *the injunctions of God's embodiments on Earth*—His Messengers? When will they learn the sacredness of each of their missions? When will they return to the Knowingness of their hearts and Soul that all lives are filled with life *only because God has gifted His Love and Spirit of Life* to each creature He created? When will humanity rise as One, indivisible Unit and say, *enough is enough*—it is time to act our age, the age of maturity—the age of understanding that we are each less than moving dust, and yet uplifted by God's Grace to exist as emblems reflecting His Image and Beauty?

There is not much time left. The Earth herself is groaning, once again, under the weight of the abuse of humanity, within itself, and towards the members of the animal, plant, and mineral kingdoms.

The Native Americans understood how the web of life hangs in a balance below the sight of the Great Spirit, the Great Mystery. The aborigines knew that each day on the outback was a precious gift given by Divine Oneness. There is no separation within all life. As all *the Embodiments* have said, we are One Body, One Tree, One Sea of Awareness filled with infinite tiny points of entry—back to the Soul—and forwards to a fifth-dimensional state of Oneness, the fifth-dimensional universal mind contains the Spirit-portals to worlds upon worlds of God, the proving grounds for our advancement towards, or regression from, Paradise: realms of perfection and nearness to God.

Let us beg our Creator for forgiveness, and, more importantly, let us determine to make closeness to our own hearts and Soul—the reflection of God within—to be the most important objective of all our thoughts, feelings, and actions.

Let not our petty differences of opinions distract us from this most important objective.

What do we have to lose? Our mortal lives will end as they have always ended, and we (our spheres of awareness integrated within physical units) will continue on to other lives in other worlds inside the Simulator. What will we have to show for them? As God sees into each of our hearts, as we wait to be tested by the touchstone of His Justice, tempered by Mercy, what will He see, within the world of time?

Will He see an entity whose life exhibits the virtues of compassion and love, justice and mercy? Such an entity He will Return to that one's True Self in the Immortal Realm of Perfection, Paradise.

Or will He see an entity whose life has scattered destruction, as a storm wind scatters leaves and branches, and fells innocent trees? The sphere of awareness of the latter being will continue the journey within the

33

Simulator—through worlds of birth, death, separation and suffering far from the Will and Pleasure of God.

It is your choice, oh, humans. Choose wisely, and choose well.

The Earth has a deadline before sanctions will be imposed.

The All-Merciful will not allow her to suffer indefinitely.

Choose wisely, oh, immortal ones, known as humans by agreement. You have been warned. Choose well.

CHAPTER 7

THE RISEN

EXPAND THE TIME. ENTITIES, KNOWN as human by agreement, have been arriving here on Earth over its history long enough to give us a picture where we find ourselves in great cycles of development that begin well, then end in great disasters. In fact, these disasters are so cataclysmic that they erase any trace of human presence or involvement. Our recognized history is based on the physical evidence from recent archeological discoveries. The history of human civilizations is far older than this evidence suggests.

Many ice ages, and other upheavals and disruptions upon the planet, have occurred over an immense period-of-time, eliminating the evidence that would have given us a different perspective. This point of view is one where we, as humans, are more directly involved with the changes we now think of as evolutionary in nature; instead, we are directly involved in the rise and fall of civilizations, as well as the balance within and among the mineral, plant, and animal kingdoms, and the human biological unit.

In our attempt at being god on Earth, we have controlled and manipulated outcomes so that the results that have manifested in our present civilization *give the appearance* of being simply adaptive, environmental changes as part of a process of evolution without any previous human intervention.

It is thus very difficult for present-day scientific inquiry to arrive at any other understanding than the one being upheld as our most accurate representation and model of the human presence here on Earth. Moreover, we are also ignoring the probable effects of outside intelligent influences over that same period, again, occurring over such long periods of time as having left little evidence, or speculative interesting traces at best. Such multi-species, intelligent interaction, would have carried very interesting results, especially when we consider a larger Plan towards Remembering and Returning—in which each entity's attempt at both enlightenment, and integration of Soul and Spirit, signals the ultimate progress.

We have not thought, so far, of an all-inclusive history involving us all as a species within a Simulator, growing Spiritually and having all sorts of challenges that bring about progress or regress in terms of our individual or collective remembering why, or what, this fractional and temporal, existential experience is all about.

There is no history long or accurate enough, or replete with the right evidence to shed light upon a different history, one different from that which is insisted upon today, based on physical evidence presently available.

There is nothing wrong with the latter approach, for as long as we realize that there is a whole much larger than the one we have explored, to understand ourselves in the context of our planetary environment. Our present understanding requires knowing our larger purpose and direction. We have a common objective that we are all a part of, regardless of how many eons we are able and willing to include in our scenario. To be accurate, the scientific perusal of *humanity's* field of activities must include the range of journeys—our dreams within a the Dream—that have occurred over endless periods of time.

We have yet to seriously address subjects such as our own immortality, returns (incarnations), and other worlds of God embedded and layered omni-dimensionally, offering multi-directional outcomes as journeys within a Simulator. We have yet to comprehend the loops that trap an entity in repetitive sojourns when she or he fails to come to Self-Knowledge, as consequence of poor decisions during the transit, and transcendence from one to the next condition of existence. We live, thus, bereft of a complete history, and lacking a better understanding of the human experience.

We remain perplexed and intellectually fragmented at best, not a pretty sight or a situation that invites hope at arriving anywhere soon enough to signal a change in the right direction.

Physical evidence has its merits within a certain time and place, just like a Revelation from God dispensing divine energies that are time and place specific. The whole process simply proves that change is inevitable. The need is there to connect certain dots outside logical, mind-dependent, and direct reasoning, a type of reasoning that is insufficient when dealing with a reality no longer circumscribed by the outward physics our dream-journeys ascribe to.

There is much more information we ignore, or that falls outside the periphery of our attempts at inquiring into an understanding that is all-inclusive. Much is left outside the realm of true possible outcomes. Prejudices and short-sightedness have taken their toll over the centuries, and in certain areas of inquiry they have imprisoned our true development. It is no surprise that these Divine Luminaries, as Representatives of the Creator and Ancient Travelers, say each and every time upon arriving, how *far behind they find the inhabitants of this planet in their on-going development.*

Due to humanity's lack of capacity as a species, the Manifestations of God therefore discarded, or were prevented from revealing Divine Information that as creatures would have moved us much closer to our Creator, the One, True God. These Messengers were left no other choice but to repeat again Teachings earlier Dispensed.

Like students that must repeat the same grade in school, the human race has been kept back in its Spiritual progress, being unable to reach the grade that allowed for a more complete perspective of the purpose, direction, and significance of our existential journey!

Who should we blame for this condition? Where do we direct our attention for this colossal mistake, an oversight that keeps repeating itself time and again, especially when so many Messengers have come, and continue to arrive, over the same period.

We can blame no one else except those entities that have come, explored, and experienced this Earth, and have tried to possess that which cannot be had, or be taken with them, beyond the confines of their fractional, and temporal, sojourns. In their attempt to play the roles of gods, these entities become less than human.

There is little doubt that those entities, known as human, are simply lost within themselves, with little hope of change. No matter how many times the opportunity to walk through a Portal invites and offers them freedom from the blind choices that trap them, bringing about the loops that imprison their Soul-based awareness, few are the ones that reach for the Knob that opens that door, and walk through.

In the depths of the Mystery of Divine Love is a kernel of Truth, a concentrated nugget of Light, we must cling to. This nugget is the assuredness, within each of our own hearts, that God loves us, always.

This certitude transcends any temporal conditions or time-periods. Without this certitude, nothing in life makes sense. With this certitude, the length and breadth of infinity encloses each of us in its warming embrace, forever.

In order to find and experience this certitude, one must dig deep, like a miner, to find the gold nugget of Surrender, tempered by the mallet of Fortitude, and washed in the stream of God's Forgiveness. *With these qualities, one can cling to the Hem of the Flowing Robe of Love and Truth of the Manifestation,* and allow one's Self to be pulled, gently, into the meads of Perfection that Paradise represents.

There is no other way to His Love.

What we are coming to realize is that there are two ongoing activities mutually compatible, operating in tandem, and feeding cohesively to form the many structures and functions that run one complex System, the Simulator.

These two components present themselves everywhere and at all times in two formats, the one that is sense-perceived as the effect of the other one that is invisible. These two, the seen and the unseen, whether near or far, within our universe or elsewhere, reflect together the quality of all decisions and activities, all the interactions and exchanges taking place everywhere within Creation, and automatically carrying out the required adjustments to preserve its integrity and purpose.

The unseen is observable to entities whose ever-advancing, omni-dimensional, multi-directional states of Soul-based awareness allow for the opportunity to serve civilization. These highly evolved Beings participate and interact with others tenth-dimensionally, in order to bring about the intended results within the Divine Plan.

To us, experiencing this third- and fourth-dimensional fractional and temporal, existential experience, the whole appears to follow certain recognizable patterns that bring a gradual completion of an understanding related directly to our various levels of capacity. As our capacities increase from greater Knowingness, we, as humans, will act upon intentions based increasingly on the greater good, rather than upon intentions based upon selfish desires.

As the inhabitants of a particular planet progress in their knowledge of third-dimensional, sense-perceived structures and functions, and in their Knowingness of unobservable conditions within the fields of activities permeating the whole (the Spirit- and heart-based fifth dimension and above), their actions increasingly counter the errors from the past, made by them as traveling entities.

Regardless of previous intents or agendas, by individuals driving the distortions that brought destruction through conflicts, wars, famine, disease, pollution, cross-contamination, and economic disparity, society-as-a-whole's greater capacity and understanding of the multi-dimensional Reality, run by a Creator outside His creation, can become an orderly unit functioning within the guidelines (commandments) of His Eternal Plan.

As more and more entities progress in their understanding and Knowingness of what now appears to be hidden and unobservable, all the adjustments will begin to be carried to create a new pattern, a shift in the conscious-awareness of all.

Within each individual, the True Purpose of existence will be Clarified and strengthened, along with the real significance of the Simulator as a training ground for each being's relation to the True Self, to the True Self of others, and to the One True God.

Individual entities are already carrying out missions to implement these adjustments and changes, effecting gradual modifications to the on-going events that would otherwise derail the progress of this civilization's attempt at surviving.

In tandem with those entities, who as handlers are participating throughout the many worlds of God, overseeing the growth in understanding and its applications, those endowed with their true missions ensure that the Divine Plan is carried out to completion, regardless of human resistance, cooperation, ignorance, etc., this time around.

The time has come for that Day of Enlightenment that is not followed by the Night of error and perdition we have grown so accustomed to experience. The Day of God is here, as He Who is Lord of all the worlds has Proclaimed His Summons.

When the sound of the Trumpet calls, the people have an opportunity to respond. They can choose to listen and to obey the injunction of God's Messenger, or they can choose neither to listen, nor to obey, and to remain within worlds of suffering and delusion.

This Trumpet call has been sounding since the mid-eighteen hundreds, in this new cycle in human history. That time period runs through 2094, a grace period given to humanity to follow the Commandments, and surrender to the Will and Pleasure of God.

Is there anything which you, as an individual, immortal being, can change in your life so that you may become the harmonious, balanced, loving entity that you were always meant to be? Is there any change in your conscious-awareness that you can effect in order to surrender your life to the greater harmony and wellness of the Whole? Now is the time to take action for the good of all—which is the good of your own Higher Self.

It is your choice.

When activities which appear to be negative happen, there is a reason. Have faith that that which is right will prevail. *"God works in mysterious ways"* is a saying that illustrates that point.

Whenever an activity will prevent something for the greater good, that activity is blocked from completion. Life is ultimately designed to achieve God's Will and Pleasure, though on the surface results may not always appear so.

Trust in God, and all will be well. That is the maxim for all time and all spiritual conditions.

We need to remember and recognize the Highlights of our lives—those moments that stand out in the narrative of each of our existences as being especially notable. Near-death experiences, dreams that foretell future events or forecast the results of conditions of certain personal situations—these are all Highlights to alert and inform us to the way Reality is truly functioning in our lives.

Without these unique events, we can get lulled to sleep, spiritually-speaking, and forget that each of us is an immortal entity existing at the tenth-dimensional level, while projecting the Soul-based awareness to the fifth (Spirit), and the third (physical) dimensions, resulting in the fourth-dimensional (mind) understanding most live by.

Highlights are gifts from Higher Realms to remind one of the Love always emanating from Source, and to jump-start our appreciation and gratitude for God's ocean of Love which He pours upon us when we offer even a single, tiny drop of our love to Him.

Highlights define our lives as spiritual experiences resulting from the inner focus within each of our hearts upon the portal of Love which God is ready to open for each of us if only we were to ask—with gratitude and humility.

Like a lantern swaying in the night at the top of the ship's mast, the Highlighted moments of our lives cry out for recognition: the *"Here I am, Lord"* moments breaking through the traps and delusions of fractional, temporal existences to form, of the rough clay of our lives, the brilliant cloth of gold, woven of the Noon Brilliance of the Day of God, spelling in golden letters:

> Here I am,
> Thy Servant
> To Thy
> Master Plan.

Let these moments inform the very threads upholding the cloth of thy existence, so that thy life shines, with the Beauty and Grace only the All-Knowing One can bestow.

Think of it this way, even the right thoughts that are meant to guide you towards enlightenment, owe their existence to the Beauty and Grace of God, the Creator of it all. To invite the right questions, the way leading to those important existential answers, we show our appreciation and gratitude to God as our acknowledgment that everything begins and ends with Him.

When we state that everything begins and ends with God, we mean that as written. As each of our states of Knowingness gradually increases, each and all travelers come to realize that within and without the Simulator there is nothing but God.

Imagine then, how it all looks as we embark in these fractional and temporal, existential experiences, denying and/or ignoring this fundamental verity?

Wouldn't you say that <u>*being lost within your Self*</u> describes such sojourns well?

Such is the human plight, totally lost within one's Self without knowing or feeling that something wrong is going on. Worst yet, you are bereft of those moments of clarity, those chance meetings within your Self to ask the right question, because those questions never come.

Not believing in God, or denying outright His existence, and participating in His creation, comes at a price. When you get lost within a labyrinth of possibilities, you are truly without a guide that can show you the way out—those solutions that can end the turmoil and suffering, giving you as the traveling entity those breathing moments of <u>*hope*</u>.

Without hope, humanity is subject to all the maladies that a condition of distress brings about: from depression to anxiety, addictions to physical illnesses. Medical science can hardly keep up with the number of cases of dis-eases that pop-up here and there, wherever a small or large community of travelers have gathered to interact and experience life.

The signs have always been there. We are not getting the right questions because we have distanced ourselves from the Creator of it all.

In the material world, where energy transitions to matter and matter to energy, the Soul-based state of awareness remains unaffected. Only our perception, our focusing, is changed. When pure awareness is translated in transit—and integrated—with the physical form, we begin to focus outwardly. When we "*leave*" our bodies, and "*return*" conditionally towards the tenth-dimension of the Self, we re-initiate an inward focusing from the **heart's portal of God's Knowingness and Love**.

This process mirrors each entity's creation **from within** God, being given "*awareness*," and **moving outwardly thereafter** to create the illusion *of separation from that Source*. There follows an immersion that assembles **the Whole into a part**, one's Being; thus one becomes aware of one's *I*-ness and being-ness, only to initiate **from within** a journey that takes each of us **from without**, time and again, to worlds that can serve as unified systems of intelligent life within a Simulator, for our development, Remembrance and Return.

This Love and Knowingness is the only true perspective with which to understand life.

The dreams within the Simulator that we are brought-in to experience, within God's Dream for our-Selves, reveal a facsimile or likeness that reflect our hearts' purity, an ever-changing reality superposed and made a seamless part of a physical system, within a universe, within a galaxy, and within one planet we think of as our home.

These fractional and temporal existential experiences turn into an illusion as we return the focus of our awareness—to our-Selves, so that from within we open our eyes one last time as immortal entities unto the Dream of God.

In order to remember our-Selves as eternally existing within God's Dream, we have only to remember one Truth: He does what He Wills and Pleases. This remembering allows each of us *to let go of the hold an illusory life* may have upon us, and focus on our inner Knowingness as directed by God's immutable and perfect Will and Decree.

Serving that Remembering is the rock of Truth upon which the Lighthouse of Knowingness is founded. As we bow our wills based upon personal desires to the Grand Design of His Vision, we find our fulfillment within the Spiritual Heart, and awaken into eternal life.

At the moment when the physical body is left behind, as our state of pure awareness retreats towards a fifth-dimensional Spirit state and portal, we each experience a shift in domains at the "*heart*" of the Self.

At this time, the increased amount of bliss and light submerges, and overwhelms the entity who is approaching the moment of *waking up* to the true condition of the Self as an Eternal Being, experiencing the coalescing effects of Reunion and nearness to God in His Paradise.

Were the entity, who knows only of his mortal condition, suddenly to become cognizant of his or her true Self, the experience would be too shocking for that entity in human form to continue existing within the physical framework.

It is for this reason that we develop and return at our own paces, in a gradual approach to the Reality of each one's True Self.

Pray to the One True God for enlightenment—an opening of one's heart as a portal to higher realms of nearness to our Creator—in order that you may be given the grace of "*lightness of Spirit*" that will lead you to your tenth-dimensional Light Body of joy. This condition, existing within your own heart, which it-Self is existing within the Heart and Mind of God, makes the worlds of dust irrelevant, at best.

Thank God for His Grace and Mercy. He illumines who He Wills and Pleases, and has destined for each one of us, at the proper and divine timing, a Life of perfections, lit by the wisdom of each and every One of His Manifestations.

When the time comes for each human entity to leave his or her body (to die), the process is simple, though the means to that end may not be so. The sphere of pure awareness withdraws gradually from the body (the third dimension), to the level of the Spirit (the fifth dimension), in a reversal process. The sphere of one's Soul-based awareness is then launched forward again to a more progressive, or regressive, world corresponding to the level of spiritual growth that the entity has attained through the use (or not) of virtues in the previous fractional and temporal life.

Were we each to remember our True Selves, we would each return to the Soul-based state of awareness, exit and awake, as entities with a Light Body, eternally bathed in our Creator's Love and Compassion. Let's be clear that when referring to a "*Light Body,*" we are addressing the fundamental differences that exist between the conditions of each entity's existence when awake in the Reality of God's Kingdom, and when asleep in the Immortal Realm and awake only to the dream-worlds of life and death in the Simulator.

The more we hold on to the material realm, or even the fifth-dimensional realm of the Spirit, as traditionally understood, the more we are held back from returning to our Selves (or higher nature) within our hearts. When we do not allow ourselves to experience the necessary purity and surrender, we are not able to return and dwell within the Inner Paradise.

How can we accomplish that return? How can we let go of the reins of selfish passions and cling to the hem of the robe of guidance of the Prophet? These questions have been explored in broad terms, in this, and previous, books. In specific terms, it is necessary for each individual entity to follow the Voice of the Manifestation of God as It touches the heart, awakening each of us, through God's Grace, in that placeless Realm.

The reader must be aware that even this interest, and the associated thought-forms, come from the Creator. This means that if you are not interested, or these type of questions do not come to you, God is withholding them both. Without the motive power, and/or the right questions, the answers that can break the cycle that engulfs the traveler will not appear.

We thus invite all traveling entities, regardless of age, place of origin, gender, or language spoken, to read the Word of God made available through His latest manifestation, named Baha'u'llah at this time, and experience for themselves the effects of the Word of God in their lives—the Faith of God, or God's Faith in His Creation.

When the entity, human by agreement, reaches that stage of evolution where he understands that the Will and Pleasure of His Creator is the determiner of his life, he is able to move forward, from worlds of physical life and death, to worlds where the transition is measured in degrees and quality of light—Love and Beauty.

This emanation of Light from the entity's core (Love and Beauty), or Soul-informed sphere of awareness, is a reflection of that being's purity of heart and sanctity of mind. These qualities are determined by the degree of closeness and devotion to God as His presence is revealed through the Word of His latest Manifestation.

It is for this reason that the golden key to one's spiritual development is the Book of that Prophet and Messenger sent down by God to *en-light-en* the people of Earth, as they carry out the narratives of their fractional and temporal, existential experiences.

God is the judge of each of our efforts to approach Him in nearness, heart to Heart, and mind to Ancient Mystery.

CHAPTER 8

LIGHT AND SHADOW

O NLY THOSE WHO WANT TO *"ascend"* need apply. If you pay attention, you will awaken there.

At this point in time there is a sacred word invoking, and connecting the creature and the Creator; that word is, *"Baha."*

Entities keep on returning to mortal realms simply because their hearts desire to do so. Their entire fractional and temporal, existential experiences revolve around a third-dimensional world construct: pursuing, avoiding, getting attached, interfering, blocking, loving, hating, and being angry, jealous, envious, busy, or not. So many forms of involvement leave little or no time for paying attention to God, the way this act needs to be done.

The results are a lukewarm, erroneous understanding that never brings about the needed enlightenment and integration, causing, upon departure from a particular mortal life, the lack of attention or focus necessary to latch onto one's higher Self's state of awareness. Instead, the individual awakens once again, in another world earmarked as fractional and temporal. This world provides a physical body allowing the entity *once again* to participate in those existential experiences, that hopefully will encourage the proper response to the *Clarion Call of the Beloved*, the Remembering and Returning this time around to the True Self: an immortal Light Being living in Paradise in the Day of God.

If, on the other hand, the entity remains lost in the quagmire of self and passion, and does not respond to the Call of God's Manifestation, he or she will keep on returning, again and again, to worlds within the Simulator. The effect of inattention to what liberates, and paying attention to what incarcerates, is that the traveler is kept in loops that continue to entrap— one's immortality at work in lower-dimensional worlds.

The way in which we modify, adjust, plan, and concoct each of our realities expresses and reflects our inner integration of the Soul-based awareness and its physiologically-based consciousness, as we explore, discover, and advance through worlds within the Simulator.

One way to become less attached to experiences based upon material realities is to develop the ability to leave the ordinary sense-perceived realities behind, through so-called *out-of-body* experiences. Perceiving from a fifth-dimensional, or higher, awareness can increase the range and scope of one's understanding. During those higher-dimensional interactions and exchanges, as omni-dimensional and multi-directional potentials in transit, in short sojourns, we can experience journeys of Remembrance and Return to the Source.

This ability also may be used for the practical intention of developing applications that enhance, and/or resolve issues of importance in the present day. These issues would otherwise be too difficult, or impossible, to solve, as is amply demonstrated in the following story....

The writer knows of one case where a scientist, with over two thousand patents in his name at the time, disclosed how he was able to travel, time-forward, to worlds where technological advancement exists. This ability gave him the opportunity to examine and utilize discoveries that could be applied in our world today, given our less-developed state of knowingness.

Such an example of out-of-body experiences shows a use of one's abilities to travel, backwards or forwards in time, for the benefit of those sharing a particular frame-of-reference, and residency, in time and space.

Out-of-body experiences have many applications: from hovering one's state of Soul-based awareness locally, to moving farther away to experience a region, planet, galaxy, or universe within this track of time, or to crossing into parallel, unified systems of intelligent life.

Elsewhere, and while hovering the point of view, we may participate in worlds so different that their uniqueness offer to the traveler opportunities for Self-growth beyond our present capacity to understand. These, and many other opportunities, are encompassed within God's Divine Plan for His creatures.

Unfortunately, most people are only conscious of limited, third-dimensional results obtained as a by-product of competition, greed, and untrustworthy and immoral means; furthermore, these results, *rewarding* the few, are falsely justified by spacious promises of national *security*, or *survival* for the many.

Instead of the promised peace and security, these wrongly-intentioned activities bring about a tug-of-war between nations that results in destruction, suffering, and death. Moreover, coupled to the costs accrued from a debt caused by military spending that overburdens the social structure, an economic imbalance is created world-wide that makes it impossible for people to maintain healthy, happy lives.

Such is the case when entities deprived them-Selves from interacting and experiencing *a Whole* that would set them free from their limited understanding and prison, a loop that has, and continues to have, a hold on each and all of them—prisoners of their vain imaginings and mismanaged passions and ignorance.

There is so much information to share that the writers feel the burden of creating a narrative so vast in size that few will feel the interest to navigate its pages and understand its content. It is for that reason we have maintained brevity, leaving the bulk of the information and experiences for a later time. Perhaps then, conditions will be suitable for presenting this information in person, through conferences, with pertinent questions from those entities willing to transcend and ascend to the rest of the story.

This story, the authors may add, assists all travelers in obtaining a broader understanding that illumines the purpose, direction, and significance of their personal journeys. Collectively, when we look at the parts as being contained within the whole, we can perceive an overall view allowing the opportunity to *peek and poke* at the Divine Plan of God, in minute ways. Yet, this view is broad enough, at this time and place, to give each of us a sense of the immensity of such an undertaking, its implication throughout eternity, and, our great responsibility and obligation to join in this eternal endeavor and mandate: to serve an ever-advancing civilization.

Many other are the cases of entities whose transiting potentials, as Soul-based states of awareness, move through and across domains to witness and experience events outside each being's time-track and planet.

Tulpoid images (partial materialization), or ghost-like appearances can occur; that is, visiting entities can acquire the necessary *reality-density* to interact with, or be observed by, entities (such as human) who are fully materialized physically upon a particular planet (such as Earth).

The non-physical entities hover their states of Soul-based awareness and attain thus the ability, to a certain degree, to interact with others living on the planet.

In short, travelers are simply moving their points of view along tracks of time, and/or crossing over spatial boundaries to attain entrance to other dimensional viewpoints—allowing for inter- or intra- transit to occur.

One of the authors has had these experiences, as well as has come across other entities, whether in the role of a male or a female, that have narrated similar stories. Time may be slowed down or accelerated to suit a situation, allowing the participant to know in advance of an event, or to avoid an undesirable event. In other cases, a person, persons, or even an occupied car may dematerialize when necessary, allowing those involved to escape an untoward event such as an *accident.*

Such an array of conditions exist that the observer/participant is required to shift points of view in order to comprehend how, like light and shadow, the seen and unseen sides of realities overlap within the Simulator.

Among other experiences occurring within the nature of this dream-reality, that help us to understand its range and scope, are those cases where a body is home to more than one point of view; that is, the body is subjected to multiple tenants. This is the case of a Brazilian healer, better known as Joao de Dios, who, when asked about his healing abilities, said that three former physicians (now deceased) took over and used his body to perform successful surgery on others while he stood hovering nearby.

The human body is just an instrument made available in this world, housing the Soul-based (awareness) point of view and allowing the traveling entity the ability to explore, interact, and exchange with others, while serving an ever- advancing civilization.

These and other phenomena point to the nature of the dreams within the Simulator, allowing for infinite possible outcomes throughout journeys in and out of myriad worlds. Developing and growing in understanding, the spiritual traveler thus remembers, and eventually awakens to, the True Self living in Paradise.

This awakening, coming to, or returning to, one's Self is dependent on the recognition of, and obedience to, the Manifestation of God, whose presence in all the worlds of God is the Portal, the point of entry, allowing each of us to Remember and Return from our journeys of separation.

When the happiness quotient of humanity is gradually incremented, automatically problems disappear. The Love of God produces incredible bliss that fills every particle of every cell with the Light and Joy of Paradise.

This Bliss is only available through the Grace and intercession of God's Manifestation upon a particular planet. It is therefore incumbent upon each entity to put forward a full effort towards discovering the Manifestation of the Day and Time in which one is experiencing a particular experience in a particular location in a universe.

One's destiny, as ordained by God, is to radiate His Beauty and Love, in service to all sentient beings everywhere. *A very good destiny for each of us, is it not?*

At the time of transitioning, signaling the end of this sojourn, when the physical form is left behind, the sphere of awareness that gives each of us our point of view is gradually withdrawn from this world, transiting through another point of entry, to be gated in and out to another world. For this reason, it is important to keep one's point of view focused on God and His Manifestation, obtained through the latest Dispensation of Divine Information. Were one to lose one's focus on God at the last moment of one's mortal life, the next step in one's eternal journey could be just another world within the Simulator, rather than the eternal Realm known as Paradise.

According to God's Will and Pleasure, each Soul-possessing entity travels so spiritual growth can be continued. The level of growth is, as previously said, determined by the purity of the heart. When one recites the prayers, out loud or silently, given by God through His Messengers, the heart becomes purified, and the mind is aligned with God's Will and Pleasure. Thus, one has the best chance to obtain the minimum standard allowed to leave the conditions of the Simulator, and ascend to the immortal Realms of nearness to God.

During every transition back to the True Self, the entity confronts the state of radiance of the traveling heart, in comparison with God's Radiance living within the Eternal Paradise. The results of such a realization bring about great joy or great sorrow. By coming to, or moving away from, the focus of attention upon the Self, the Being of Light either awakens in Paradise, or acquires again a consciousness of mortal worlds within the Simulator.

This cycle repeats itself until the entity is finally able to release his attention and heart from all else except God.

It is for this reason that we must continually remind our Selves of the true reason for all of our journeys—to return to the One Who created each of us from His infinite Love and Compassion. In order to express that which He desires us to express, our Selves as perfect mirrors of His Image and Beauty, always mindful of the Great and Lesser Covenants that guide all travelers seeking the Truth within Creation, we must always be alert, listening to His Voice.

It is important to understand that during the time when an entity, known as human by agreement, is experiencing a fractional and temporal, existential experience, his or her awareness can combine with physical consciousness, and be consciously aware of the Whole.

When the Soul-based point of awareness is released from consciousness through physical death, the ability to Remember and Return to *Full Knowingness* is hampered by the inner state of one's heart when impure. It is during that potential in transit, the transition between worlds, that God gives each of us, according to each one's capacity and spiritual station, the opportunity to Remember the Love and Wisdom that we, as immortal entities existing tenth-dimensionally, have always had.

The concern is that, should our attention, or the focus of our points of awareness, be focused upon things other than God's Will and Pleasure, we will each return immediately to a world within the Simulator, be given a body suited for that environment, and each one's sphere of awareness, its range and scope now limited, will conjoin and acquire a state of consciousness.

How may we prevent this regression and prevent returning to worlds within the Simulator?

Again, divine Love is the Key. By purifying the heart, during each fractional and temporal sojourn, the entity is potentially enabled to awaken as his True Self residing in the Paradise of God's Love.

By reading the Word of God, from His latest Manifestation (the Glory of God), for the day and age of the entity's emergent sojourn upon the shores of consciousness, the heart and mind of the traveling entity may become purified enough through the bestowals and blessings of the Creator's Word for that entity's ascent; that is, upon physical death, that entity's awareness will be allowed to remain with the Self, functioning in an immortal Realm outside the Simulator, in service to, and in accordance with, the Will and Pleasure of God Almighty.

Blessed is that state and station!

Not all paths lead to God. Some path are detours—seeming to lead towards Him, while, in fact, leading away towards perdition and error.

How do we distinguish those paths that lead towards higher realms of nearness to God, the Creator of all, and those that lead towards worlds of birth and death, physically-speaking?

When the heart is pure, one will be led automatically to realms of Light that accord with God's Will and Pleasure.

So purifying the heart becomes *the key factor* in creating a condition of understanding from which the entity may choose the right—and righteous—path.

The Word of God, unsullied by ecclesiastical interpretation and pseudo-spiritual leadership, performs this service of purification—read the Book yourself.

CHAPTER 9

IT IS WHAT IT IS

THE ENTITY'S STATE OF *KNOWINGNESS* in matters of the journey: remembering and returning, one's spiritual development, the purpose and direction, and its significance, remains up to God's Will and Pleasure to illumine and advance.

Without God's Illumination, you do not understand that what you know and that degree of knowingness becomes the cage that holds you prisoner at all times, causing you to be your own worst enemy. It is a quagmire you cannot free yourself from, no matter what you may hear or come across. Without God's given Word, through His Messenger, you will never understand it, and there will be no interest or reason to do so. You will, in fact, be lost within yourself and not even know it.

Individually and collectively, generation after generation, most of us have continued this same pattern of unawareness, as we transit *from one to the next dream* (world) *state*.

We are trapped in a loop that is both the Whole within the Self, and the part within that Whole, each time we emerge to its surface. Each time we experience a state of consciousness, we become trapped in one of the many fractional and temporal, existential experiences held from within, and experienced from without.

The entity has no recollection or memory of these fractional and temporal, existential experiences. Gradually, as the entity accrues virtues through the practice of ethical values, and a morally correct life-style, he or she experiences moments of clarity, fourth-dimensionally speaking, and is guided, discovering the Manifestation of God for the day and age of his or her emergence into a theater of life.

This gradual process is part of one's awakening, remembering, and eventual return to one's higher Self.

When the entity finally awakens and returns to Paradise, fully aware of his true Self, all thoughts and memories of former (dreams of) mortal worlds vanish. His attention is now focused on that which God, in His Infinite Mercy and Wisdom, has specifically designed for that particular entity.

Since the entity is in an eternal companionship, the experiences of both entities will be coordinated to fulfill the Desire of God, the Creator, to carry out His Will and Pleasure.

Whenever an entity leaves behind the worlds of illusion, they vanish without a trace—as a tiny drop of water vanishes within an immense and immeasurable ocean.

Were you, the reader, to have this experience of *leaving* the physical body and experience these *Realms of Revelation*, you would soon understand that nothing in this primitive world of time and space, life and death, with a diverse lack of attributes, has any true value whatsoever.

The only worthiness found in these worlds within the Simulator is that they should remind the interacting participants (through their Soul-based awareness) that God is All There Is, for everything else is experienced as a vanishing point of view—eventually.

Were it to be revealed to most of the people interacting and participating on any planet, as a unified system of intelligent life, the Beauty and the Joy eternally available in the Realms of God, all the persons sojourning there, would cease *the moment to get to the Other side.*

For this reason, most of humanity, in particular, has been kept in the dark in many ways by the Emissaries of God, in order that all could continue their journeys within Creation, perfecting their Soul-possessing Spirits, gradually.

Now is the time to awaken to this realization (understanding), and to know the full range of God's Love, Mercy, and All-Knowingness. Now is the hour for all hearts to be fulfilled through the Nation of Glory, serving the One True, Living God.

In this way the Name of God rings true within all the entities' hearts, activated to bring about the Heaven of Gloriousness. <u>That point of view becomes the pathway to God.</u>

The gradual integration of one's Self, during the journey of *Remembrance and Return*, precipitates a number of phenomena that carry very interesting special effects. Among these is the super-positioning of realities, where transformations to an existing environment take place.

These transformations, where the *revealed beauty* of a higher, more developed realm interacts and superposes its state of beauty over a less developed one, accent such phenomena.

These and many other experiences highlight the entity's transformation as he or she gradually ascends and becomes the channel of the divine flow ever-present in higher Realms.

In a lesser way, and just as important, is the influencing beauty expressed through the creative mind, finding its way through the arts and music: This influence is another example of a super-positioning, in transit and in effect from one to another world of God.

When we consider being within a Simulator that anticipates all human activities, as it replicates our hearts' desires, the creative beauty accessed through those entities whose nearness to God proclaims servitude, realizes the evidence of His existence.

The opposite is just as evident, when such nearness is absent, in one way or another. The further the entity's heart's desires are from the True Beauty of God's Love, the less likely any manifested action will reflect the Beauty of that Divine Realm.

Observe the contrast between what is right and what is wrong, what is beautiful, and what is not, reflecting the purity of the heart of a social order whose members have degraded their hearts. Realize how such a gradient of diverse states of purity reflects in the world. Moreover, what is right or wrong, beautiful or not, carry those effects to their fruition, yielding lower gradients of beauty, and undignified behaviors not in harmony with the station of servants of God—yet, those who practice such behaviors do not understand their consequences!

Just as we need to be educated in order to understand and properly function in society, in a social order, which grows more complex over time, technically advancing as its people explore and discover, we require spiritual education, the kind that takes us into those higher states of Soul-based awareness, in order to complete the human experience.

Human entities are, too, in need of a Universal Educator to adequately understand and participate within the Dream-world state accorded to their needed advancement and journeys on the shores of consciousness.

Without this education, and Divine Educators, humanity cannot integrate and obtain a conscious state of awareness, the complete understanding of God's Divine Plan for all earthly travelers sojourning, intent on exploring and discovering a way to Remember and Return to their True Selves.

Just as earthly education is vital to everyone, divine learning, too, is essential to the entity's Spiritual well-being; without it, the entity becomes lost within his or her Self. The dreams within the Dream become nightmares, fractional and temporal existential experiences leading the traveler back again to other worlds. These mortal worlds may be experienced in the present tense, or through later sojourns of returns, as the entity is given further opportunities for introspection and Self-development.

Such is the nature of one's fractional and temporal, existential experiences, either allowing the progression towards one's higher Self, until the Being's awakening, or producing a regression into the labyrinth of the Simulator that knows no end or beginning, the entity unable to Remember or to Know.

Both earthly and divine education complement and serve humanity in its achievement of results that liberate and advance the social order, by assisting the collective integration into more complex circles of unity.

This oneness and unity continues within and among other life experiences, on other planets, within other unified systems of intelligence. Each entity thereby obtains experiences that complete that entity's development from one to the next moment, as a continuing potential in transit and transcendence, until finally the Being of Light awakens in the Higher Realms of Glory.

The entity's sphere of awareness has then returned as the True Self in Paradise.

Such is the Divine Plan of God, meant to orient and guide all the traveling entities towards a common objective as servants and participants in a Grand Design. We are in need of illumination. In turn, we continually obtain the enlightenment that sustains a Soul-based state of conscious awareness, bringing cognizance of both temporal responsibilities, and their impact on our eternal existence.

When an entity *incarnates* (integrating the sphere of awareness, the *Soul*, with physical consciousness) upon the Earth, or any other planet, there are no memory residuals to speak of. The Soul-based state of awareness (tenth dimensional) cannot be remembered consciously (fourth dimensional). There is only the positive synthesis of accrued attributes present as innate potentials (fifth dimensional), at-the-ready for further development.

When a Manifestation of God comes, it is an opportunity for those sojourning on the planet to receive the necessary education and upgrade their conscious understanding. The wisdom, resulting from practicing alignment with this embodiment of a Perfect state of Soul-based Awareness, allows humanity to Remember its own Perfection within the endless Dream of God for each Soul-possessing, Spirit Being of Light (life and intelligence).

At this time, in the history of Planet Earth, there is an opportunity for all the members of the human race to discover the Word of God in the Writings of His latest Manifestation. Thereby, they each may obtain the perfection of the heart so necessary for Returning to one's perfect Self, the state of awareness of one's divinity as expressed consciously upon the planet.

For this Self-awareness for each member of humanity we pray—and give thanks.

Humanity is entering a crucial phase in its collective maturing process. It is time to get serious about the way we approach the responsibilities granted during our stay on this planet. There is little time—astronomically speaking—left to address our state of Knowingness.

Any system of life, no matter how simple or complex it is, has a certain amount of time to show how well put together its components are. The human race is no exception.

A new cycle of maturity for humanity has begun to express its unseen content, and bring about the necessary scientific advances (such as computer technology) that will materially unite the human race. This physical bridge propelled by our science, *underlined: unless supported by an equal advancement of the human heart*, will prove unsustainable and catastrophic.

We are beginning to observe and experience the inherent power within the early baby steps our science brings. We are also observing and experiencing the missteps made with our technological advances so far.

There is a time given to stop a species' effort to destroy its own kind, and its environment; we need to act now, before the consequences of the denial of the creatures of their own Creator—and His Divine Plan—bear the bitter fruit of planetary annihilation.

This realization is not a warning, nor a misguided sign of the times. It is a clear part of a collective process inherent in any, and all, closed systems. It is a safety subroutine built-in all unified intelligent systems of life. Life promotes life; death promotes itself. Life guides life towards another day of living. Death removes all vestiges of inadequacy and failure over time.

Moreover, entities without the proper spiritual advancement, their Knowingness and Lovingness, cannot progress into higher Realms. The doors are closed, and in some situations, for a very, very long time.

Staying in worlds that begin and end is not a welcoming scenario, regardless of content. The time each entity has within one mortal life amounts to very little. When the entity's sphere of awareness is no longer coalesced with its physical consciousness associated with that one life, the individual's memories vanish. Without memory, the individual's historic narrative can repeat itself, over and over time, with no way to stop it except through an infusion of Divine Energy (the Holy Spirit) from higher realms—outside the Simulator.

Your immortality at work!

CHAPTER 10

GOOD AND EVIL

INSOFAR AS THE UNSEEN AND the hidden, the concept of *good and evil Spirit* beings points to an interesting dilemma, an ever-growing world as a remnant of these contrasting influences. The question is whether this third-dimensional construct is, was, and will continue to be, inhabited by those fields of imperceptible activities dominated by good—or by evil.

When the heart of each of those traveling through the many worlds of God remains empty of God's Love, His Divine imprint, that entity's Soul-based awareness becomes exposed to evil influences. As the landscape of human activities grows in the absence of the Love of God, so do the malevolent and malicious influences and their varied immoral manifestations within the theater of life. Moreover, within the Simulator, the traveling entity's experiences *show-and-tell* of the heart's state of purity. The environment reflects, in its beauty, or lack of it, the effect of the hearts with, or without, the Love of God. In worlds like this, where good and evil coexist as the result of the gradually increasing presence, or absence, of His Love, what are the consequences for each sojourner within God's Dream—and Divine Plan?

There is an ever-present struggle going on, a tug of war within the Simulator, within every unified planetary system of intelligent life. The fields of imperceptible activities (within the fifth dimension of the Spirit), representing good and evil, come to the forefront of all sentient activities to demonstrate the consequences of a world dominated by the divine –or their opposite—as the collective struggles to survive.

The more evil the thought or action of an entity is, and the more that entity succeeds in manifesting its iniquitous presence, the harder it becomes for all beings to move forward individually, and collectively. The more the rejection of God's Love, the more hearts that are emptied of His Grace and Mercy, the more difficult it becomes for an entity, and a world, to turn around towards the right path.

As the traveling entity forges ahead, pursuing evil and vain imaginings, he or she finds it increasingly difficult to exhibit the innate, positive qualities of the True Self within, born out of the Love of God, Creator of all that is good.

All traveling entities are, herein advised that the time has come when these two imperceptible fields of activities, the Spirits of life and death of the heart, must be consciously confronted; the time has come to make a conscious choice towards, or away from, the path aligned with God's Divine Will and Pleasure.

This is the Day of God, a Day not to be followed by the night of error, relentless passions, and evil imaginings that have for so long ruled this planet. The task is at hand, and the call is given.

Good shall prevail, and the Love of God will conquer every heart!

Oh God, my God. Grant that the day is soon approaching that all Souls may be blessed with the Presence of God united within the mantle of God's protection and forgiveness, blessed by His Wisdom and Insight, so that His Divine Will may prevail in all situations. Moreover, throughout all times for the good of humanity and of all the worlds upon worlds throughout His Creation.

Grant through Thy Mercy that each one may return to the Life of the Soul-based spirit, filled with the Love of God throughout eternity, and with no desire except to fulfill the Will and Pleasure of his Creator.

Grant through Thy infinite bounties that each being may attain to his or her true Purpose—to fulfill the Dream of God for the immortal Soul and live forever within His Will and Pleasure.

Within this cycle of humanity, there is a choice to move forward towards God, or backwards away from God. There is no in between.

The choice is determined by the purity of the entity's heart. Should the heart be greater than half-pure, the being moves to higher realms closer to perfection, upon the death of the physical body.

Should the heart be less than half-pure, the entity descends to lower realms of more contrast, further from God's perfection, upon the sphere of awareness leaving the physical body.

At this special time in the history of humanity, the Manifestation of God for this time-period—Baha'u'llah—has been given the authority to assist those of pure heart to advance towards the Lord of all the worlds. It is for this reason that it behooves each entity, with a conscious-awareness of this planet, to embrace the injunctions of All-Mighty God, as given by His Latest Messenger.

Were there another way to purify one's Self, and advance towards the re-uniting with the True Essence, it would have been revealed. So follow the path that has been given, and shown to assist in the obtaining of the true blessings destined for each, and every creature made from the Creator's divine clay, animated by His breath of Life.

Let nothing stop thy search for the True One!

Otherwise, the entity lives trapped and encapsulated within his or her state of Knowingness, its range and scope addressing third- and fourth-dimensional orbs of understanding, only.

Through Education, traveling entities are enhanced, and are able to understand, the world around. The deeper they are able to focus, explore, and discover, the greater their depth of development will be.

The spiritual state is open for exploration and discovery at all times and to everyone. However, the illumination that allows for such exploration and discovery is God-given.

Here lies the answer: God illumines the heart of whom He Wills and Desires. Thus, all entities remain entrapped by their Knowingness until God Wills it otherwise.

Such an entrapment brings about the ignorance (not knowing), and suffering we are all familiar with. Additionally, our lack of understanding of what the journey is all about risks its greatest objective—to awaken, finally, as our True-Selves, and end these fractional and temporal, existential experiences that invite only the taste of life, not allowing us to keep whatever was obtained during those short sojourns.

A life of contrasts earmarked to test and challenge all travelers to Remember and Return continues, assessed from within, and guided from without. Cast into a whirlpool of choices, not knowing from where it all began, or where it will all end, the entity must reach for Divine Guidance, Mercy, and Love.

To invite the Love of God, the traveling entity must love God first!

The purpose of all existence is to return to God, it's Creator. There is no other purpose. This eternal goal is achieved, through the Manifestation of each day and age, regardless of external circumstances—such as from which world the creature of God is in the process of returning. Without this forward motion towards the Essence of Infinity, the creature, and the world inhabited, is filled with the sorrowful decay of a dying world and a life-less Soul.

For this reason, it is advised that each creature, each immortal entity searching for the Cause of that immortality, should put forth a penultimate effort to discover He Who represents God in the day and age in which that entity is existing in physical, material form in a mortal world of dream states. No other Cause is worthy of pursuit, and no other goal will allow the entity to achieve the pre-destined Perfection for which each Spirit Being of Light is born eternally to fulfill.

Good and evil doors are available. Which do you choose? Portals that lead you closer to, or further from, the True-Self? To do the right thing, or not? To serve others in ways that assist their understanding and their lives, or to use the moment to take advantage of someone's generosity? To help educate humanity and assist in bringing the results that advance an eternal civilization, or not? To live the Love that bonds everyone and everything, or to deny Its existence and live experiencing the emptiness of disappearance?

The choice is always there. Choose well, fellow traveler.

When integrated from within—the Soul-based state of awareness with the Spirit Being of light, mind, and body—the journeying entity within the Simulator's worlds upon worlds has the capacity to recognize the Manifestation of God. This recognition occurs because the engraved Image of God and His Revealed Beauty come together from within and from without—the most contrasting of all symbols found in a dream-state within a Dream.

Whenever a Manifestation of God "comes to town," the local inhabitants are given a chance to enliven (come to Life) from within the Soul (become aware of), and awaken to the new, deeper levels of Knowledge that are brought in. Without His coming, they are not given the opportunity to ride the Light Rail to its destination in the Realms of Immortality.

It is for this reason that we urge the inhabitants of this time on planet Earth to strive with the utmost effort to free them-Selves from the shackles and blinders of past misinformation and limited understandings. We urge the chargers of their intellects and hearts to gallop towards the open arms of God's Representative for this time, as He opens the Gates of Paradise to the true and truthful seeker.

Many are called to respond to the Clarion sound.

Were it not for the intercession of the Messengers of the One, True God for the peoples of the Earth, this planet, and all that lives upon it, would have disappeared into oblivion many, many ages ago.

As the Words of the latest Manifestation of the All-Knowing One, *since the year sixty (1844)*, are been translated into many languages, it is incumbent upon every true seeker and servant to read and meditate upon those Words. They are like gold, which when polished by the soft cloth of the loving, understanding heart, reflects the wisdom that cannot be tarnished by the ravages of time, or the chances of destiny.

These golden Words light the unburning fire within each sincere heart, so that an understanding blossoms of Reality the like of which can only be imagined from the viewpoint of one attached to the dust-filled pursuits of mortal, dream-world states.

Were each man, woman, and child upon the Earth to make the study and understanding of the Words of God given to the Blessed Beauty, the Being who represents Him, every entity upon the planet would respond and arise in Joy and Wonder to proclaim:

"God is most Glorious. Praise be to God!

The root of all evil is found in a heart where God is absent. The entity with such a disconnected heart soon discovers and experiences the nightmarish dream-states within the Simulator through the many conditions of separation from the Creator.

We must remember that in a beginning that knows no beginning, God created the human race in His likeness—engraved with His Image and animated with His Spirit of Eternal Life. It is for this reason that He expects so much from His human creatures. They each were created with the stamp of His Hand saying, *"This Soul-based awareness is Mine"*.

When we allow our Selves, who we really are, to forget our Divine origins, we not only descend to an unspeakable level below that of the instinct-based animal, but also close the door of the *tunnel of Light* that instantly connects each one of our hearts to the Infinite Source of Love and Compassion.

Without being fed by His Love, we become like beasts roaming aimlessly around the desert, no grass to graze on, and no well to slake the interminable thirst.

Just a small, a very tiny, step towards the Creator-of-All's Love, from within the Heart of the True Self, is necessary to send our hearts on the infinite and infinitesimal journey back to the True God who created the spark of each awesome entity from the unburning fire of His Love and Compassion.

Take that step, dear one of Planet Earth, holding hands with each sibling, each of God's children, and watch the planetary hell become a luminous realm of paradisiacal Love.

CHAPTER 11

THOUGHT-FORMS

CREATION IS THE EXPRESSION OF a *thought-form,* in a timeless and space-less environ, within an eternal Source and Essence we have come to be aware of as the Creator—God. Our Soul-based awareness, God-given, is at the core of our relationship with, and dependence upon, He Whom God makes Manifest.

Nothing else matters. Here lies a beginning which knows no beginning, and knows no end—a mystery that becomes known to us through Himself, as an aspect of His Will and Pleasure to those He alone chooses to Illumine.

What we come to Know is a reflection of His Will and Pleasure.

All else that is known through our own wills vanishes with our deaths, after each fractional and temporal, existential experience—the journeys of separation.

Whatever becomes Known to us about Reality is, first and foremost, Known to He in Whom that Source is Manifested. He is thus the first Soul, the first Spirit, and the first Mind—the Perfect Instrument that makes available His Will and Pleasure.

To understand and acquiesce to the supreme importance of God's Manifestation requires submitting one's will to His Divine Will and Pleasure. To fail to have and understand this viewpoint reveals that one has yet to be chosen, and remains among the unguided, lost within the self.

It is that simple. You are either illumined, or you are not. You either Know, or you do not. Pray to be one of those that Knows.

Those that do not Know live in a mind-state that breaths with discontent and confusion, a world of questions that roam freely within, making reference to a third-dimensional disorder without rhyme or reason—until eventually these questions are tossed aside, unanswered.

Many are the wise men and women who have set aside this approach as they each explore and discover how difficult it is to find the answers required to bestow satisfaction and tranquility to their hearts and minds.

Many have compensated for their inner emptiness with half-answers, superstitious practices, rituals, and even traditions passed on to their children, (who, in turn, do the same) until, little by little, these hand-me-down practices lose their significance and are left behind.

We were created with the ability to introspect, to look and think about the created, to form opinions, to arrive at scientific verities that have been probed and proven to repeat themselves often enough to be understood as factual—until something else expands our horizons of knowingness.

Our dream-states within the Simulator make it all feel *real*, a bio-feed-back that happens to be at the core of what is experienced, and is so closely embedded within that it certifies and gives a repeatable familiarity to what is taking place from one moment to the next. The longer each being lives in this fractional and temporal, existential experience, the more firmly that individual's belief becomes absorbed as part of that third- and fourth-dimensionally-based *reality*.

Trapped in that bubble, the traveler finds solace in a balloon community, whose existential bubbles (the spheres of awareness of other travelers) share aspects of community experiences as they each reciprocate time, and again, with others; until the moment comes when they must depart and no longer be present to continue in the same theater of life.

This is a simple way of explaining life on earth: a merry-go-'round of activities, multi-directional in their outcomes, interfering or merging at times with other outcomes, in order to bring about conflict, or progress, as the end result.

When the entity becomes disengaged from his or her Soul-based state of awareness given by the Creator and Source of all that is, the severed entity's sojourn becomes a nightmare. This solo trip into unknown realities make available a disarray of possible outcomes, not connected with the *Whole of Life*; the Being of Light is steered off-course through the power and manipulation of egoic desires and environmental forces, moving the entity further from the true goal of nearness to the Beloved.

One's physiological-based consciousness serves as both a window onto, and a monitor to study and reflect upon, the world of matter. Information (data) is first uploaded and experienced third-dimensionally. When this information is understood through the fourth-dimensional state of mind, time, and energies, the resulting mind-world construct defines and houses the traveling entity's summary of all the memories of his fractional and temporal, existential experience.

At the other end of the spectrum, one's Soul-based state of awareness offers a portal that connects and brings one's attention to a Reality that contains the Revealed Beauty of the Creator, perfections manifested over an eternal continuum.

The coalesced mix of two distinct, and quite different, realms, united through God's Love, influences and brings about a mind-set affecting the way we perceive and behave in the temporal world, and preparing us for our ultimate destination.... By overriding all focus on Earthly objectives, and paying more attention to the World to come, we may, with God's Grace reach His goal for us.

Experiences from that Realm come when we are ready to receive them, and that decision is God's alone.

No one can shorten the time it takes to bring the moment of enlightenment to bear its fruits. Your Knowing, or not, has a purpose, like everything else, to bring you closer to your True Self, and thus to allow you to experience Reunion with the Beloved of all the worlds.

When an entity's Soul-based state of awareness and first point of view leaves the physical form upon death, the process of Self-retrieval is initiated. The being's viewpoint moves away from the dream-state, and the most recent fractional and temporal, existential experience, into the next life-experience and chapter.

The direction of this *movement*—or change in Spiritual state or condition— represents the accumulation of all the increased values of all the virtues practiced in the most recent sojourn.

The context of these values gives a perspective on the *worthiness* and *Reality* of that entity's identity as a servant of God the Creator, and becomes a part of the traveling entity's *sphere of pure awareness*, a chromatic resplendence of light of greater or lesser intensity, depending upon the degree of purity obtained within the heart.

In order to gain the greatest degree of attribute-development that serves as the heart's Spiritual development, the traveling entity must first surrender completely to the Will and Pleasure of the Creator. This surrendering itself is dependent upon God's Will—for without His assistance the *ego-modulations*, attachments of the entity to the material world and concomitant belief systems, are too strong of an obstacle to allow the weak-willed creature to follow the lead of the Creator.

For this reason alone, it is strongly suggested that each entity, upon entering a fractional and temporal, existential sojourn, search with all sincerity for the One Who represents God for that day and age.

That One is the *golden key* to an understanding of the intricate levels of Reality engulfing all travelers that exist—both from within creation, and outside of the *Simulator* in the Realm of Revelation—the infinite worlds of God.

Pray heartily for the Knowingness that will allow one's heart to expand with God's Love that encompasses <u>all</u> realities, beyond any and all restrictions of time and space. Pray for illumination, always. *God illumines the heart of whom He Wills....*

In preparation, the *seeker of Truth* must nourish the growth of the *Tree of Life* within the heart—to seek the Love of God.

Its *Roots* are plunged into the soil of men's hearts. The branches stretch up into the sky of *heavenly knowledge*. The sap is the breath of the holy Spirit of Eternal Life, the Breath of God, breathing life into all of Creation. The Tree glistens with the golden light of Divine Inspiration.

The nightingales sing the songs of the Immensurable Heart—the Love flowing like an ocean from eternity to eternity. The Light of Divine guidance illumines the sky between the branches, as the newly-risen Sun illumines life everywhere with a fresh impetus, a newly-created Revelation of Peace and Tranquility, emanating from the One Who serves the One, True God.

The swirling galaxies are lit with a new Light—all Realms shouting the praise of the All-Mighty One in every corner-less bend.

The Day not followed by night has come! For this Grace let all rejoice and be thankful. There is no greater grace from God, the All-Merciful.

There is no greater gift.

When the entity, *a Light Being as a potential in-transit*, retrieves its point of view, and the focus is homeward bound within the True-Self, insofar as its pure sphere of awareness, it has the opportunity to re-align the heart with the Creator's Heart.

It is as if the drop has returned to the Ocean, the point submerged within infinity. All divisions cease in the Unity of one Amity and Accord. At this juncture, the individual entity is no longer distinguishable from the Whole.

God then decides the next step of the infinite journey for that entity.... Will the entity's sphere of awareness remain with the True Self as a Being of Light in the immortal realms? Or will God return His creature to the Simulator again, to endure another fractional, temporal existential experience with a specific mission, in order to augment the ardor of the creature's Love for the Beloved.

Only God knows the Truth of each one's heart. Only God determines the fate, the pre-ordained journey, of each of His creatures.

For this reason alone, it behooves us to open the portals of our hearts, to allow God's Love to flood every particle of our Beings, as the morning Sun floods the Eastern sky on a cloudless summer morning.

If we allow the nourishing warmth of God's transcendent Love to overwhelm our lives, our lives will make a sea-change towards unity, and grace.

Blessed be each humble servant who realizes this truth—then acts upon it.

When this Love enters the heart of the servant of God, he or she becomes the River, the channel to receive the divine information necessary to uplift the life of that servant.

This is the gift of the Source of All. Pray to be that channel, that recipient of divine information, the blessing of the ages.

This Love is pure, unadulterated ecstasy. It brings a state of continuous joy felt through each activity, in relationships, work, or simply watching nature in its many forms.

Let each moment in the eternity of existence be a celebration of the Divine Blessings from God. Let each moment be filled with the Joy of discovering thy divine purpose mandated from God, and pre-ordained since the beginning that has no beginning.

Let each moment be a discovery of the Joy of Life, encapsulated in that moment, that spark of existence, that tiny explosion of knowingness.

Let each moment be a bowing to the Oneness of Life, the awesomeness of the Mystery that cannot be fathomed—the Creator's Unknowable Essence.

Let each moment be, then, the Essence of thankfulness to the One Who brought everything into existence, the One Who even now, each moment, Knows what lies in the depths of each heart and mind….

Praise be God.

Whenever the latest Manifestation of God arrives, the inhabitants are given an opportunity to mend their ways, to change. Killing, raping, embezzling, and all other sordid acts of a depraved populace are no longer seen as "normal." The Perfect Being, in the physical form of a human, the Representative of the Great Mystery, brings *an infinite and penetrating Light to mortal darkness.*

Without this Light, humanity would stumble around in the darkness without relief. With His presence, and Sacred Writings, the imports of the Divine Voice can uplift generations to come. In order to understand, generations of humans have combed over the Writings of each Messenger. Yet they miss the point. These Writings cannot be understood through the use of the mind. Their meaning is perceived through the Soul-based awareness at the ***heart*** of who we are.

Each individual traveling entity is allowed by God to comprehend that which he or she is ready to know and experience. Purity of the heart is a factor, as well as the unknowable Will of the Creator—at the center, or essence, of who we are.

The knower is placed in a condition equivalent to his or her spiritual growth. No amount of external human learning can help. In fact, that kind of third- and fourth- dimensionally based learning is a hindrance.

Only God's choosing to open the heart-based Knowingness of His creature can assist that servant to follow the divine way given by God's Messenger appearing on Earth.

The infinite Light is lit within the heart of each immortal entity. Follow that Light within, or risk losing one's very reason for existing.

Remember, each time that one enters, in awareness, into a fractional and temporal, existential experience, one's True Self, the immortal entity that remains in a potential transit-state, connected to the Supernal Realm, is unaffected by any experience, <u>except</u> insofar as the virtues obtained during that lifetime. Thus, all other experiences that do not contribute to the acquiring of said virtues can be counted as a waste of time.

Still, in some other way, every experience has some merit in the scheme of things, and only God knows the ultimate reckoning for a life. We must do the best we can, clinging to the divine Word, and praying to be released from the selfish desires that keep each of us from reaching our divinely-ordained potentials.

Just as every day on Earth contains a sunrise, following nighttime, every *day in the life of the Spirit* contains those moments of clarity that bring more light after a period of darkness, or lesser understanding.

Watch for those moments of illumination—when the heart is filled with the Love and Knowingness that can only come from one Source…. Those moments are like golden keys opening the doors to the endless possibilities available to an entity who is awakened in the realms serving God.

This awakened entity knows neither fear nor anger, jealousy nor envy. This entity is content within the Self, with a heart filled with the ever-present, ever-lit, Lamp of Service to the Creator of all creatures. This entity *Knows him- or her- Self* as nothing—the Creator as everything.

This *Knowingness* is all there is to Know.

It is important to understand what this existential journey represents in the overall process: an activity that takes each of us from the *whole to the moment, or moments*, within each fractional and temporal, existential experience, and, at some future point, takes us back again to the whole.

Knowing that what moves from *there to here, and back again to there*, is our ***first point of view***, *as observers*, allowing us to have these many fractional and temporal experiences from a ***second point of view***, *as participants* in those dream-states, or fractional and temporal, existential experiences.

From a tenth-dimensional state of awareness, Soul-based, connected to the *Supernal Realm and the Mind* of the *Whole*, each of us transits and comes to a Universal state of mind, the Spirit and fifth-dimensional state of awareness. The fifth-dimension, as fields of imperceptible activities, allow us to connect to this precursor engine of all that is to be manifested, mentally and physically.

Finally, we each rest our focusing on the individual mind, fourth-dimensionally speaking, accessing the third dimension (on a planet such as Earth), that allows for an interactive participation as entities experiencing life within the Simulator. We are thus moved from the Whole to the moment of a fractional and temporal, existential experience.

Can we remember and return to the Whole from where we came?

Here we find the basis of all that is wrong with us. We have disconnected ourselves from our-Selves, and the resulting myopia and distortions are the effect. We are trapped in a moment, a fractional and temporal existential experience, regardless of how long that moment may be. Whether one nanosecond, or one hundred years, ***that moment is only as valuable as one's ability to remember it***.

That moment, as a *thought-form*, represents all that you are during that time-track, a fraction of a Whole you cannot remember, and thus, cannot return to.

Yet, as a matter of fact, the Whole is in the part, and the part is in the Whole—the seed and the plant. The entity, whether aware or not, carries *the Whole* as it transits through myriads of worlds *as an observer*, that become *parts of that Whole, when participating.*

As difficult as this concept is to comprehend, at first, the fact remains, you are not moving physically (a body) through these distinct and separate conditions within the Simulator. You are a *potential transiting* through as a **sphere of pure awareness.** You are Soul (a point of view, an observer), that travels within the Simulator and emerges once-in-a-while, through a process that integrates that viewpoint through stages, until completed, as part of a body that now gives the entity a *physiologically based* state of consciousness allowing for participation in such a dream-state, a world we term material, as a third-dimensional construct.

Whenever an entity becomes disconnected (cut off) from within, and is thus unable to keep the Whole coalesced with the part, such a fractional and temporal, existential experience refracts and becomes distorted, bringing about the type of shared world we have all come to experience. This refraction of the Light illumining the fractional and temporal sojourn is due to the rubbish creating a corrupt environment fifth-dimensionally, as the Spirit animating the All no longer allows the free flow of the Light emanating from God. The bending of the Illumination from the Source (through a corrupted medium), gives way to distortions, in turn bringing about the disunity of thought-forms and the absence of the Love of God.

Humankind, as a race of traveling entities, is no longer able to bring about the unity and oneness that sustains life on the planet. When the Creator's creatures are living in the darkness of their selfish desires, unguided and without the Light illumining their hearts, they find themselves separated from God. Time and again, they find themselves succumbing to the nightmares of satanic imaginings, and the chaos that ensues thereafter.

CHAPTER 12

THE WAY

Let each entity throughout Creation find the way to God through the illumination of His Source, His Messenger, for the Day and Age of the emergence on the shores of consciousness. The Sacred Words of the Prophets and Chosen Ones of God are the portals illumining the way of Remembrance and Return. There is no other way to be released from the third- and fourth dimensional realities (the traps), while the focus of the sphere of awareness is sojourning the dream-states, and the many world-constructs, encountered within the Simulator.

The Words of God break the entrapment of the mind, a fourth-dimensional thought-construct, and even the entrapment of the universal mind, fifth-dimensionally present, as sunlight on water breaks the surface with sparks of light.

Left to ourselves, we cannot see outside the bubbles of thought-forms, the mind-constructs retained as memories, identities, and identifiers built from perceptions and intellectuality. With the aid of He Whom God has made Manifest, we *once again are able to see from within our hearts* illuminated by the Creator's infinite Love and Wisdom. This literal *lifeline*, transferred from His Mind and Heart through His Manifested Representative, is that which can pull all entities back to our origins as immortal Beings, connected through the Soul to the Mysterious Essence that has neither beginning nor end.

Holding to this *life-line* in the midst of the many dream-states we find ourselves trapped in, God's Grace is what allows each entity to remember and return to Paradise within, a state-of-being composed of the ultimate surrender of one's very essence to the inconceivable, unknowable Essence of All, a Portal of Entry that admits absolute dependence on God for one's eternal existence.

Thus, the purpose of life is served when the creature recognizes its station as being both *absolute nothingness* and in a state of true poverty in relation to the Creator —the Unknowable Essence permeating from within. But for the Creator's infinite Grace in creating the creature and his surroundings, there would be no existence and therefore no purpose. It behooves the reader to contemplate this point, that is, to spend some time asking for illumination from God.

We have become so busy with the details of our lives that we fail to remember that our lives are simply dots of light lit by the Love of God.

He holds each point of light and entry into His Creation in the Palm of His hand. He watches over each tiny sphere of awareness with infinite Patience and Love, waiting throughout eternity for each of us to wake up to the realization that our *true home* lives within our hearts—within His Heart. Nothing else matters, for as we offer our hearts to the All-Compassionate One, and we bathe in even a single drop from the *ocean of His Love*, we are left emptied of all except humble gratitude.

The way is then illumined by *the Spirit of God* through His latest Manifestation. The Elucidation and Knowledge emanating from He Whom God made Manifest, shows clearly the purpose, significance and direction each and every traveling entity's lives must evince while in the service of God's Divine Plan, the ever-advancing of a True Civilization.

When we educate our Selves and serve each other, bringing an overall improvement to the way things are, in non-competitive ways, and in agreement at all times, peacefully moving forward, collaborating. and being of assistance with the right intentions and attitudes, a clear mind and a pure heart, interacting in long lasting relationships, whose participants look forward to meeting each other again and again, this moment, as a fractional and temporal, existential experience, is well-lived.

These fractional and temporal experiences, as dream-states, are meant to provide opportunities to Remember and return to one's Self, awakening in Paradise. With that in mind, the whole system, the Simulator, operates as a unified intelligent system of life, layered and embedded into a oneness built around season-like stages, where its Spring represents the period following the appearance of a Manifestation, generally lasting some two hundred fifty years. During this stage, the Simulator seeds the *S.O.I.L.* (system of intelligent life) with greater capacity and opportunities for advancement.

Following that period, its Summer, the fruits of that endeavor are expressed by all entities throughout Creation, as evidence of their interaction within the Divine Plan of God, the Creator. During the Autumn season, a purification time follows in preparation for Winter. Spiritually speaking, Autumn is a period of contemplation and introspection expressed by those traveling during this time period following the appearance of a Manifestation of God, as philosophies, a looking back and reassessing of humanity's history for its achievements and its failures.

Winter is a period experienced as a contrast to the former strength of Summer. Society-at-large feels the effects of the separation from the Divine Source, and the impact of that moment is found deep within each traveler, if connected, preparing the way for the Return of He Whom God makes Manifest.

This scenario runs within cycles, each lasting some one thousand years, more or less, marked by the coming of a Manifestation of God, Whose introjection signals another stage of development within the Simulator—a practice run.

Cycles of development are contained within a Mega-cycle, lasting thousands of years. These Mega-cycles together form a Super-cycle of spiritual development measured in millions of years, where hardly any travelers are ever aware of its conditions and eventual purpose.

The objective of these various processes, acting upon all traveling entities during the many sojourns within the Simulator, is to *squeeze every ounce of impurities and imperfections* from within the Soul's state of awareness, from within its essence (the heart). Such an eternal journey, omni-dimensional and multi-directional, is like an oven cooking every creature to perfection, a process of bringing every creature near the Creator and closer to fulfilling His Divine Plan.

This is all that can be said at this time. A process that is living proof of His Omnipotence and Omnipresent Power throughout Creation, a Will-full and Purposeful intent bringing all His creatures back to a Realm accommodating His Dream, a Paradise intent on carrying out His Pleasure.

When an entity is born into a material existence, having its state of awareness coalesced into a physiological state of consciousness, this connection and integration is dependent upon that entity's relationship with God's Representative for the Day and Age of that traveler's emergence on the shore of consciousness and plane of existence.

Without that connection to God's Manifestation, the entity soon becomes lost in the bewildering phenomena of sense-perceived occurrences. This myriad of contradictory patterns within the Simulator clouds and brings about *the fog* of ignorance, and the loops that entrap the traveler.

To drag one's Self out of the morass of environmental stimuli, coupled with genetic tendencies, and the self-serving desires of an egoic nature, is well-nigh impossible. One's True Self lies abandoned in the tenth dimension, while one's awareness focusses upon illusory happenings of third- and fourth-dimensional content.

The only answer is to cling to that Reality delineated by the One Who Represents God, the Creator of All, much as a person drowning in the ocean must cling to the line thrown to him with all his strength.

This is the Law of God, His Rules, and His Creation. There is little choice in this matter.

And yet—because there is no death—one may choose to drown in the selfish pleasures and sufferings of these material and temporal experiences, only to re-surface with one's awareness integrated with a new consciousness in a new physical unit, on a new planet, in order to continue the journey towards reuniting with the True Beloved. The only question remaining speaks of the quality of that type of journey, long with much pain and suffering, or swift and filled with the flavors of surrender and obedience.

When the entity's Soul-based awareness is retrieved from the Simulator back to one's Self's heart, tenth-dimensionally in a state of oneness with the Divine, there are no contradictions nor problems. Those perceptions that were once focused outwardly (within the Simulator) upon the illusory, material worlds, and created an experience of *separation* from the One that created all realities, are no longer in existence.

From the point of view of separation, God is seen as far and hidden. From the point of view of Unity, we each remain united with each other—and our Creator—within the infinitude of Love and Perfections in which we, as immortal entities, always exist in potential.

Which point of view do you choose? That of illusion, or that of Truth? Even choosing illusion does not destroy the immutability of Truth.

Choose wisely and well, oh servant of the One, Unknowable Essence.

The immortal entity, a potential in transit, in transcendent enlightenment, traveling through fractional and temporal, existential experiences, must eventually come to eternal life. Its Soul-possessing sphere of pure awareness, retrieved from the Simulator, awakens to an existence of endless bliss.

This state of bliss is a gift from the Creator's Love—as He keeps each of His creatures close to Him in the infinitude of His Heart. Were each entity to remember the True condition of the Soul-based state of awareness—filled with an inexpressible Love that knowns neither temporal ends nor dimensional limits, all entities would be capable of carrying out the Divine Will and Pleasure—always and only.

It is a question of *memory*. Do we choose to remember the Plan of God for each of us, embedded deep within each of our hearts? Or do we choose to focus upon the cursory, film-like images from this or that *physical lifetime* spent within the Simulator?

The choice is up to each of us.

Understandably, not everyone that reads this invitation will fully understand its import. In order to comprehend it, the entity must receive God's illumination. This observable fact and occurrence is full of meaning. On the one hand, it tells each of us Who is in control, and on the other hand, there is a reason why we are held back from *Knowing*.

What is of importance is the cognition derived from being held back. Why would an entity be held back from understanding any crucial bit of information? Is it because not *knowing or being ignorant* spells disaster, pain and suffering for that individual and for others?

Individually, the entity undergoes a stage where his or her attention meant to focus from within, to be drawn inwardly, encouraging Self-understanding. If the individual ignores this *call*, refusing to look within, analyze, and make changes, his or her life will generally not improve.

Collectively, society experiences the effects of the many entities lost from within, trapped by their ignorance. Every being is meant to practice introspection to some degree, to gain Self-Knowledge. Additionally, all must realize that without God's illumination, no one can receive and implement the understanding required to solve the maladies running from the level of the Spirit, through the mental, emotional, and physical levels in both the individual and the collective.

Thus, being held back offers an opportunity for both the individual and society to reassess the conditions afflicting all lives in the theater of existence within the Simulator. These times are always an opportunity to reflect within to call upon the Creator for His assistance, and to express gratitude and gratefulness in serving His Will and Pleasure.

After all, we all want to be happy, though without knowing if what we want is what we need. There is a difference between knowing what we want and knowing what we need. The mature entity postpones what he wants and goes after what he needs. The immature entity follows his desires regardless.

The time comes, sooner or later, to seriously think about one's life, its pattern and quality, and whether it needs to be changed. If the individual traveler does not have the interest to reassess his or her life in light of a better future, there is something deeply wrong. The only thing we can manage are our moral choices. So why not pay attention to, and remember the consequences of those choices? Why not take the time to formulate the correct questions, and seek the right answers?

In the end, the quality of one's life is determined by the quality of one's heart-connection to the Creator, the Great Mystery bringing all animate life and inanimate substances, everywhere. It makes no difference whether one has gone through a particular fractional and temporal, existential experience as a pauper—or a king.

That which is measured by the Great Assayer is the quality and purity of the *spiritual station* that has been attained. From a higher perspective, the petty, fleeting concerns of each mortal are just that—petty and fleeting. Focus upon that which endures forever: love and compassion, kindness and gentleness, honesty and integrity, and above all, devotion to the Lord of all virtuous attributes. Life will then be well spent, an eternal narrative describing a journey of nearness to God, of surrender to the Beloved of All the Worlds.

Books by Kito and Ling Productions
www.loginthesoul.com

For Adults:

Echoes of a Vision of Paradise: If You Cannot Remember, You Will Return, Volumes 1 – 3

Echoes of a Vision of Paradise: If You Cannot Remember, You Will Return, a Synopsis, available also in audio.

Restoring the Heart

The Simulator

The 2094 Sanction

A Being of Light: God's Will and Pleasure.

Paradise: The Science of the Love of God.

Books by Kito and Ling Productions
www.loginthesoul.org

For Children:

Andy Ant and Beatrice Bee: With a Bonus Coloring Section.

Beauty is on the Inside: With a Bonus Coloring Section.

Bee and Fairy Power: A love Story of Care and Concern.

Fly, Fly, Louie Louie: A story of change and discovery, with a Bonus Coloring Section.

Grandma and I: A Bilingual English/Spanish story of eating healthily, with a Bonus Coloring Section.

How Alexander the Gnome Found the Sun: With a Bonus Coloring Section.

Igor's Walkabout: A story of compassion, with a Bonus Coloring Section.

Katie Caterpillar Finds Her Song: With a Bonus Coloring Section, also available in Audio format.

Saving Lantern's Waterfall: An Eco-Adventure.

Return to Paradise: Happy the Blue-Bird and Bright-Wings the Cardinal use virtues to restore the Professor's home.

The King and the Castle: Love Flies in on the Wings of Destiny. With a Bonus Coloring Section.

Printed in the United States
By Bookmasters